Also available at all good book stores

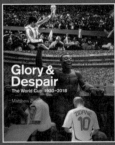

9781801501248

9781801500630

9781785317927

9781801500975

9781801500968

9781801500937

9781801500920

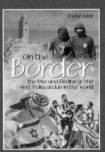

9781801500951

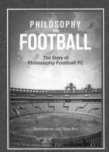

9781801501064

USA 94

THE WORLD CUP THAT CHANGED THE GAME

MATTHEW EVANS

First published by Pitch Publishing, 2022

Pitch Publishing
9 Donnington Park,
85 Birdham Road,
Chichester,
West Sussex,
PO20 7AJ
www.pitchpublishing.co.uk
info@pitchpublishing.co.uk

A CIP catalogue record is available for this book
from the British Library.

ISBN 978 1 80150 167 5

Typesetting and origination by Pitch Publishing
Printed and bound in India by Replika Press Pvt. Ltd.

Contents

For Lindsey, Noah, Flynn and Jude

Prologue

A HELICOPTER whirred overhead as a convoy of police cars scrambled to join the early-evening traffic on Interstate 5 in Santa Ana, California. Ahead, a white Ford Bronco cautiously straddled the middle lanes of the freeway. Driving was former NFL player Allen 'AC' Cowlings who a day earlier celebrated his 47th birthday; in the back of the SUV was Orenthal James 'OJ' Simpson, one of the USA's biggest sports stars, who was holding a gun to his own head.

The drama began to unfold a little over three hours earlier when Los Angeles Police Department Commander David Gascon addressed a waiting press throng. 'The Los Angeles Police Department right now is searching for Mr Simpson; he is a wanted murder suspect and we will go and find him.'

Five days earlier, Nicole Brown Simpson, ex-wife of the fugitive, and her friend Ronald Goldman were found murdered outside her home in the Los Angeles suburb of Brentwood. Nicole's estranged husband was chief suspect and the LAPD were eager to discuss his whereabouts on the fateful night. The former NFL running-back had agreed to surrender himself to the police on the morning of 17 June but suddenly seemed to have other ideas. Now he was charged with their murder, a wanted man and a fugitive from the law.

The 17 June 1994 was already shaping up to be a memorable day in US sports history. Arnold Palmer was playing his final round at the US Open whilst the New York Rangers ice hockey team had enjoyed a ticker-tape Broadway parade that morning having won their first Stanley Cup title in over 50 years. At Madison Square Garden a fellow New York sports team, basketball's Knicks, were gearing up for a vital game in the NBA finals against the Houston Rockets.

Despite the multitude of sporting excellence on display in the Land of the Free, it was presumed that the eyes of the world would rest on events some 2,000 miles away from California: at Chicago's Soldier Field, where the 15th World Cup would be getting underway. It was the first time that world football's premier tournament would be held outside of Europe and South America.

The big guns were rolled out for the opening ceremony. Chat show host Oprah Winfrey was on emcee duties, welcoming an estimated 750 million viewers to the show before she promptly fell off the stage, twisting her ankle in the process. The consummate professional, Winfrey continued to host a show which included Daryl Hall perform his forgettable World Cup-inspired ditty 'Gloryland', and an on-pitch display from Motown legend Diana Ross, who took centre stage and performed an elaborate routine for the great and the good who were baking in Chicago's summer heat.

Six years in the making and all the former Supremes lead singer had to do was hit the target. She parted the crowd, lip-synching her 1980 hit 'I'm Coming Out' in a red trouser suit, as she approached a football placed before her. A mere six yards away a pretend goalkeeper stood in front of a hastily positioned goal. Ross played to the crowd and toyed with the kick, attempting to ramp up the tension as her disco classic tinnily blared out of the stadium's sound system.

Ross eventually swung her right leg at the ball, sending it spiralling past the post whilst the goal elaborately snapped in half in a pre-planned way that hadn't considered she would miss the target altogether. Ever the professional, the Motown diva continued with the show, dancing between the dismantled goal hoping nobody had noticed what had just occurred.

The World Cup was open for business and whilst the sporting scribes prepared to detail the unfortunate mishaps on display in Chicago, the world's slowest car chase was reaching its crescendo. The 24-hour news channels had followed the parade into Los Angeles with the general public now eager to play their part in the unfolding events, some holding 'Go OJ' signs visible for the TV cameras to see.

As the white Bronco entered the 405 freeway, TV networks interrupted their scheduled programming to show the pursuit. Much to the World Cup organisers' relief, it was the NBA finals that would lose airtime and not either of the opening games. Finally, Simpson arrived at his estate grounds where he surrendered himself to a much-relieved LAPD as 24-hour news and reality television collided.

The next day Simpson stole the front and back pages of the US newspapers with some FIFA members disgruntled to see the World Cup shifted from being the major talking point. The Simpson episode had helped take some of the column inches away from Winfrey's tumble and Ross's miserable penalty attempt.

As with all news, the story moved on. Simpson prepared for the trial of the decade whilst some European football

writers were still left wondering 'Who's OJ?' The 1994
World Cup may have had its opening-day thunder stolen
from under it, but as the tournament progressed it would
have many more talking points of its own.

Introduction

THE SUMMER of 1994 saw all eyes focused on the USA for the 15th FIFA World Cup. It was sacrilege to some. Many detractors hoped it would fail, others simply sat back and expected it to. When the dust settled after four weeks of action, world football would never be the same again. USA 94 showed there was an alternative way of hosting the crown jewel of world football.

There is a common feeling amongst football fans that no World Cup holds a place in your heart quite like your first. Well, USA 94 was my third and ultimately my favourite; to me it was football in technicolour. The internet age was around the corner and USA 94 was the final World Cup where the only place you had seen some of the players before was in your sticker album.

The 1994 World Cup had it all. It was the tournament of the 'Golden Generation' with half a dozen nations boasting arguably their greatest side. It played host to the greatest collection of football's number tens, with Roberto Baggio, Gheorghe Hagi, Hristo Stoichkov, Carlos Valderrama and Diego Maradona all battling it out. There were underdogs, giant killings, a final tragedy befitting *Tosca*, whilst news of the murder of a much-loved player sent shockwaves throughout the tournament.

The misty-eyed reminiscing of Italia 90 (mainly from the English perspective) disguises the fact that the football played on the Apennine Peninsula was for the most part dull. A scarcity of goals, little action and time-wasting of epic proportions culminated in a subdued final which didn't have Los Angeles's afternoon temperatures to hide behind. FIFA had seen enough, there was too much at stake if they were serious about conquering one of football's final frontiers.

Four years is a long time in football. Italia 90 and Gazza's tears changed the perception of the game in many people's eyes. There was hope for a sport scarred by the horrendous stadium disasters and hooliganism of the 1980s as the dawn of a new decade ushered in a rebirth for the beautiful game. FIFA was already one step ahead, having awarded the USA its prized possession in 1988. Now was the time to take football to the next level, foot down, full throttle. The fate of the game's globalisation rested on the shoulders of the 1994 World Cup.

Whilst the European football press speculated on the introduction of wild and wondrous rule changes that would desecrate the game, FIFA had other ideas. There would be no splitting the game into four quarters, no ad breaks instead of action, no cheerleaders or bigger goals. Instead, minor tweaks were made which would promote attacking football. For a country where winning is everything and whose native sports generally deal in high scores, goals would be the order of the day, and plenty of them.

By offering three points for a win, it was hoped that teams would avoid playing it safe, whilst an adjustment to the offside law put the advantage with the attacker. The negative play that marred the 1990 World Cup brought about the biggest change with the back-pass rule, commonplace now but then making its World Cup debut. Aesthetically, players' names would adorn the backs of shirts allowing fans to follow suit as the replica jersey market provided another lucrative revenue stream for clubs and nations alike. Even the referees got involved in the fashion stakes with a variety of different coloured garments at their disposal. The more discerning and nostalgic football fans still mention the plethora of memorable kits – Nigeria, USA and Mexican goalkeeper Jorge Campos's attire all particular standouts – along with the huge baggy nets that hung from deep goals that seemed to go on forever.

The 'Americanisation' of the sport didn't materialise on the pitch but off it was a different story altogether. A glitzy draw in Las Vegas saw the likes of Bill Clinton and Robin Williams take centre stage, the latter stealing the show as only he could. Fans came in their droves, all more than happy to keep the cash registers ringing with purchases of an unimaginable amount of USA 94 merchandise. Some of the largest companies on earth scrambled to be associated with the extravaganza as football took its first step towards becoming the unstoppable juggernaut that it is today.

For fans in the UK, there was also an absence of home nations, a chance to enjoy the games without worrying about who would win them and a chance to adopt a team to follow (in my case I chose the hosts, convincing my parents that, yes, I did need that denim-coloured shirt resplendent with white stars). My love of football stemmed from my dad sitting me on the terrace barriers at Wrexham's Racecourse Ground as an inquisitive five-year-old, but by my early teens, I was rapidly falling out of love with the game. Having been pushed to the periphery by the cliques that so often plague junior football, it was exacerbated by a miserable high school experience where only the strongest survived. I retreated into my shell, deciding to keep my head down until the storm had passed. During the summer of 1994, the World Cup reminded me of why I loved football and how the game was a huge part of who I was as a person. When I decided to fulfil a lifelong ambition in writing a book, there could only be one subject.

When planning how I wanted to write the book I decided against a day-by-day account and instead opted to dedicate chapters to what in my opinion are the most interesting aspects of USA 94. This gave me the breadth to fully cover the best teams, and the story of the volunteers who helped put the bid together as well as the legacy left behind as North and Central America gear up to play host again in 2026. It is one that is guaranteed to take the World Cup to yet another new level, but one that without the success of USA 94 may not be happening at all.

Matthew Evans

Chapter One

How the West Won

'ANYONE WHO thinks that football isn't part of the fabric of American life is either an idiot or not paying attention,' said an exasperated Thom Meredith, a former director of communications for US Soccer. This was news to the European footballing fraternity who had traditionally looked down their noses at their counterparts over the pond when the suggestion arose that the USA would like to host the 1994 World Cup.

This wasn't the United States Soccer Federation's (USF) first World Cup rodeo. Back in 1983 they launched a rushed and unprofessional attempt to replace Colombia, who had lost the rights to host the 1986 tournament. A lightweight 92-page brochure, complete with bird's-eye view photographs of pitches with gridiron markings, did little to impress the top brass at FIFA.

The head of international football was already less than enamoured with the way that the USA's premier football competition, the North American Soccer League (NASL), had adapted and changed the laws of the game to suit themselves. The bid was shot down with disdain by FIFA president João Havelange who declared that the USA 'wasn't ready for such a competition'. The Brazilian later bestowed the honour on Mexico, who hosted their second World Cup in 16 years.

Perhaps Havelange had a point; by the beginning of the 1980s the bloated NASL's heyday was over. The glamour years of Pelé strutting his stuff for the New York Cosmos at Giants Stadium was a faded memory and the league desperately floundered in a sea of high costs and dwindling interest. Its 16-year run came to an end in 1984; football had enjoyed its season in the sun but now it was expected to be filed away whilst the USA got on with their 'own' sports.

The fact that it did not can be attributed to one man, the late Werner Fricker, backed by his passionate team of football-loving volunteers who refused to give up on a sport they came to love during their college days. 'Soccer was a participatory sport,' explained the then-USSF chief media officer Jim Trecker. 'Especially at the youth level, kids loved playing soccer. It was not an unknown entity, just not front-page news,' he continued. 'We knew these people would be intrigued enough to buy tickets, although it was a hard sell until they actually did.'

Twelve months after Mexico 86, where Argentina triumphed in a close-fought final with West Germany at the Estadio Azteca, bids were welcomed for the 1994 World Cup. As was the tradition then, the host nation would be from the Americas since Italy would represent Europe in 1990 and FIFA alternated between continents. Four bids were received: Brazil, Morocco, Chile and the USA. Brazil, the South American footballing superpower, were rapidly installed as favourites. Chile soon dropped out due to financial issues whilst FIFA had yet to risk handing their most precious possession over to an African or North American nation.

A key moment arrived in 1984 when Los Angeles played host to the 20th Summer Olympic Games. With FIFA looking on, football became the most-watched discipline out of the 29 on display with 101,799 fans crowded into Pasadena's Rose Bowl for the gold-medal game between France and Brazil. This wasn't an anomaly; the semi-finals and bronze-medal match had also seen attendances north of 100,000. Tickets resembled gold dust and FIFA was impressed; general secretary Joseph 'Sepp' Blatter was a keen observer. Perhaps the general public in America was finally getting to grips with the beautiful game. TV network ABC had paid an astronomical $225m for the rights to show the Olympics, which dwarfed the $5m that rival network NBC would pay two years later for Mexico 86. The seed was planted, the USA was back in favour with FIFA, and this time there would be nothing left to chance.

Up stepped Werner Fricker. By day he was a real-estate developer who had worked his way up to the USSF's top position in 1984. Fricker was born in Southern Banat, Yugoslavia, on 24 January 1936 to a German-speaking family. By the time he was eight, the Fricker family had fled to Austria to escape the horrors of World War II. The majority of them found work in a shoe factory where 70-hour working weeks were the norm.

By the early 1950s, the Frickers had emigrated to the USA and settled down in the Philadelphia area. Fricker learnt carpentry and joined a local football side, the United German Hungarians, where he patrolled the midfield. He started his own construction company in 1963 and was part of the US Olympic team a year later. Football remained an integral part of his life and soon Fricker joined the administration at the USSF.

In April 1987, Fricker formed World Cup USA 1994 Inc., a non-profit organisation created purely for constructing and presenting a bid. The USSF had five full-time employees and operated with an $800,000 budget. Having the volunteer force on board would be invaluable especially when it came to bridging the huge financial gap. Some $1.5m alone would be needed just to get the bid in front of FIFA.

Within this new set-up, Fricker utilised the likes of Meredith; Trecker, who benefitted from his earlier experiences with the Cosmos during the Pelé era as well as the NFL's New York Jets; California-based attorney Scott LeTellier and Rey Post. The last of these was a chief consultant for Eddie Mahe Jnr and Associates, a political consulting firm in Washington. Having been left some $1m in the hole after the botched attempt at hosting Mexico 86, Fricker was all too aware that this was as much of a political challenge than a sporting one.

Buoyed by the volunteers working around the clock, Fricker concentrated on getting the additional funds required having managed to haul the federation back to liquidity. Fricker had secured some credit lines to keep the bid on track yet there was still a significant shortfall in ensuring the well didn't run dry. In a gesture made in faith and desperation, Fricker re-mortgaged his own home to raise the remaining half of the money the USSF would need to see them over the line.

By September 1987, the bid was complete. Trecker, who had initially been brought in to cover the media side of things, had played a much bigger part than he originally envisaged. 'It was a lot simpler process than it is now, it was basically producing terms of reference. FIFA asked questions and we answered them,' he explained. 'I ended up writing, editing, proofreading and finalising the contents before it went to the printers.' One stipulation was FIFA's desire to see a new professional league in the USA and they stressed there had to be a legacy to the tournament. Post had used his political links to open the doors to government. Along with former US secretary of state and veteran of the failed Mexico 86 bid Henry Kissinger, he had arranged a meeting between Havelange and White House incumbent Ronald Reagan. Two months later 381 pages of leather-bound documentation were signed off and carried aboard a flight headed for Zürich.

By this time, speculation was beginning to grow across Europe and South America that the bid was the USA's to lose. The apparent seriousness of the bid, combined with Chile's withdrawal and a growing financial crisis in Brazil, appeared to be tipping the balance in the USA's favour. Rumours circulated that Brazil's presentation had left a lot to be desired too, even containing some handwritten sections. When their delegation was late for FIFA's Italia 90 qualifying draw, their fate appeared to be sealed by the governing body's hard-line approach to pomp and circumstance.

Stadium presentation was a specific area where the USA had upped their game when it came to the second bid. Gone were the pitches with gridiron markings and, in their place, a study of how it would be possible to replace the artificial surfaces with natural grass in line with FIFA protocol. The minimum requirement to host group matches was a stadium capacity of at least 40,000, with this figure rising to a minimum of 60,000 for the semi-finals in a city that was capable of hosting both games. Brazil's bid was in tatters; the economy was crashing with billions owed to US banks whilst their stadiums sat in disrepair. As part of the bid process FIFA sent two teams to inspect potential World

Cup stadiums which seemed to seal the deal for Fricker's bid team as the last remaining rival, Morocco, had only one stadium up to the required semi-final standard and two that could hold more than 40,000 fans.

With the bid documents submitted and the stadium inspections complete, there was little else Fricker and his fervid force of volunteers could do but wait. As the announcement approached one remaining concern was overcome when Havelange removed himself from the vote, stating a potential conflict of interest. Despite the vote being performed via a secret ballot, speculation had mounted that any votes from European federations were likely to be in the USA's favour. All earlier Latin America-based tournaments had yet to provide a European victor, so suddenly the USA was viewed as something of a neutral venue by these nations.

Still, Fricker refused to get carried away by whispers from the rumour mill. The advantages of hosting the tournament in the USA were clear: they had the infrastructure, stadiums and the Olympics displayed there was an audience for a big footballing event. Cynics and naysayers questioned whether the Olympics was a one-off and noted there was still no sign of a professional league happening anytime soon. It had been two decades since football in the USA had been branded 'the game of the future', plus the national team hadn't qualified for a tournament since 1950 where they secured their famous 1-0 win over England. For the USSF, the future was here. It was now or never if they were to ever host the World Cup.

With Havelange and fellow Brazilian Abilio D'Almedia declining to vote, only one obstacle remained. Would the other committee members vote in favour of Brazil in a sign of solidarity to their president? When FIFA announced a slight change to the date when they would announce their decision, those reading between the lines could have been forgiven for reaching the obvious conclusion. The venue remained the same, Zürich's Mövenpick hotel, but it would no longer be taking place on 30 June. Tellingly, the date had been moved to 4 July 1988, the 212th anniversary of America's Declaration of Independence.

A team of around a dozen made the trip from the USA to Zürich, amongst them Fricker, Meredith, Stiehl, Trecker, Post and future head of US Soccer, Sunil Gulati. All three delegations were invited to make a 30-minute presentation to FIFA. Brazil went first and voiced their concerns at the USA hosting the World Cup, likening it to taking the baseball World Series to the Samba Nation. Morocco was up next, they too spoke out against the USA being potential hosts, claiming that they already have many huge events and didn't need any more. Finally, the USSF made their pitch. Concentrating on themselves, they rolled out the big guns as President Reagan spoke on video in favour of the bid and promised the government's unilateral support and backing.

By noon the presentations were complete and the delegations retired awaiting FIFA's verdict. A little over an hour later the heads of each bid team were called back to receive the results of the secret ballot. Fricker left the room as Trecker, Meredith and Gulati knew that 15 months of hard work rested on FIFA's decision.

'We were waiting in a small holding room at the Mövenpick,' said Meredith. 'The door opened and Werner was stood there, stony-faced. He said, "the vote was 10, 7 and 2." That was all he said! We looked at him. "Well who got the 10?" Werner's response was so typical of him. "The United States of America." Not "the USA", not "us", but "the United States of America"!'

The result was ten to the USA, seven to Morocco and two for Brazil, who had fallen from early favourites to dead last.

As the celebrations began, a knock came on the door. A FIFA official was there, asking why the delegation wasn't at the news conference. 'No one had told us what we needed to do next, we were just so happy and congratulating each other,' Meredith recalled. 'We all left the room and ran down to the conference hall, entering breathless as FIFA's Henry Cavan announced to the world that we had won the bid,' he added.

FIFA spoke of their desire to promote the game and take the World Cup to uncharted territories. The European football press scoffed at what they saw as a potential disaster whilst the cynical amongst them spoke more of the huge commercial opportunities that the host country offered. The delegation arrived home to little fanfare from the press or public. Either way, the USA would be hosting the 1994 World Cup. Fricker, though, tempered expectations at the news conference: 'We still have a long way to go, but now we have a target.'

As the calendar turned to 1989, Fricker and the USSF devised a blueprint which they hoped would help them reach this target. They received a boost when the national team qualified for Italia 90, but their performance left more questions than answers. FIFA looked on, unimpressed with the sluggish state in which progress was being made. In Fricker, they found someone ill at ease when it came to jumping through their hoops. Finances were still an issue. Fricker had to secure more credit lines just to pay for the national team to go to the 1990 World Cup.

Fricker was adamant that the most important part of the World Cup was what it would do for the growth of football in the USA. He fought FIFA to ensure the USSF received their fair share of sponsorship money from the tournament, much to the chagrin of world football's governing body. After all, they were the ones taking the risk of handing the keys to the World Cup over to them. There was much at stake. Pull this off and there would be riches galore for all parties, on top of growth for the game stateside; fail and it would be a death knell for many involved on both sides. Both organisations seemed to be on a collision course and, as the dust settled on the USA's dire display at the 1990 World Cup, FIFA made their move.

Chapter Two

A Leap of Faith

THE CALL came in the summer of 1990 as unrest between FIFA and Werner Fricker grew. It had been two years since that momentous day in Zürich when FIFA had named the USA as hosts for the forthcoming World Cup. At Italia 90, the US national team had been an unmitigated disaster, suffering three defeats and picking up zero points. In the players' defence, the national team was made up of college-standard players and run on a shoestring. Things would have to change if they were to avoid being the first host nation not to advance past the group stages at the next World Cup. Whilst there was time to address this, it was the glacial movements off the pitch that had Havelange and Blatter most concerned, although they had one man in mind who they knew could get things moving.

Alan Rothenberg was a trial lawyer in Los Angeles who first came into contact with football at the age of 28. Born in Detroit, Michigan, in 1939, Rothenberg graduated from law school in his home state before moving to California. It was whilst serving as a lawyer for Jack Kent Cooke that he became exposed to the NASL as his employer purchased the Los Angeles Wolves football team. Cooke's footballing venture was brief and he is best remembered for three titles as the owner of the NFL's Washington Redskins and basketball's Los Angeles Lakers.

Rothenberg's involvement with the business side of football clearly had an effect as he headed up an investment team to purchase the Los Angeles Aztecs NASL team in 1980. Similar to Cooke's experience and perhaps a sad indictment to the league it was also short-lived. Rothenberg stated the opportunity merely came at the wrong time as the Aztecs folded the following year.

With the 1984 Olympics fast approaching, the Games' president Peter Ueberroth named Rothenberg as the soccer commissioner. It proved a quantifiable success with the sport becoming the most popular event that summer, even outselling the perennial favourite, track and field. It was a lightbulb moment for FIFA and the time to promote football in what was seen as the 'last frontier' had arrived. Football could work in the USA and the 1984 Olympics was proof.

Six years later, back at USSF headquarters, Fricker was about to cross FIFA once again. Finances hadn't improved. The national team's qualification for Italia 90 had garnered $1.4m but the federation was still being run on credit lines and goodwill. FIFA had done their bit, allowing the USSF to borrow against potential ticket sales, but there were still no major sponsors on board, a distinct lack of a TV deal and no director of marketing.

With money running out Fricker attempted to strike a hastily arranged $11.5m deal with the NBC for the rights to show the World Cup. Crucially he did this without FIFA's knowledge or approval, with network rivals the ABC and the CBS lodging complaints at their lack of opportunity to bid. FIFA nixed the deal and by the time the dust had settled NBC had moved on, spending that money and more elsewhere with some $600m splashed on a four-year deal with the NBA. Rumours persisted that FIFA would change the hosts, just as they did in 1986. The reunified Germany, current World Cup holders, waited in the wings with a former player, the oft-outspoken Paul Breitner, eager to tell anyone willing to listen that the Germans could step in as hosts at a moment's notice.

The relationship between Fricker and FIFA looked to have reached its nadir. The USSF president felt he had the interests of not only the federation but also the country at heart, yet somehow he failed to notice that there was a desire for change in the air. There had been growing unease from federation members who were unhappy with the progress under Fricker and his cliques. There was too much at stake to stumble now, the USSF presidential election was fast approaching, and the future of the World Cup in the USA rested on its result.

'I was contacted by people on behalf of FIFA for the role of running the 1994 World Cup. I was asked if I would be interested, to which I replied "yes",' explained Rothenberg. 'I asked what was needed and was told I would have to be elected as president of the USSF, but I wasn't even a member [of the USSF] at this point,' he added. Rothenberg officially announced his candidacy, up against Fricker and former head of World Cup 94, Paul Stiehl. The race for the USSF presidency was on, a non-member going head-to-head with two federation stalwarts. Rothenberg had two weeks to convince the members that he was the man who could not only deliver a World Cup but also make it work.

The vote was split into sections with each state association having their say alongside youth and grassroots levels. The final section would be the professional vote. As there was no professional league in the USA, this fell to the clubs who competed in the indoor football leagues. Fricker had caused consternation with them having overlooked their players when selecting a squad for Italia 90, opting instead for those with college experience.

'I thought I could get the professional vote,' said Rothenberg. 'Having experience and a background in professional sports I knew how it worked,' he explained. The grassroots of US soccer had been promised a new professional league once the USA won the bid, yet two years on there was still no sign of one. The USSF were back in a $650,000 hole, with only a credit line keeping the World Cup Organising Committee (WCOC) afloat. Patience was wearing thin; a golden opportunity was at risk of slipping from its grasp.

The election was to take place in Orlando, Florida. Stiehl and Fricker had been at odds since LeTellier had replaced the former as head of the WCOC. With so much at stake, they put their differences aside as rumours grew of the two combining to see off the Rothenberg threat. Allegations emerged that notes were pushed under hotel room doors warning against a vote for the newcomer. FIFA responded, reaching out to delegates on the eve of election day urging them to vote for Rothenberg as the real threat of losing the World Cup became even more evident.

The 583 votes were cast, verified and counted. Alan Rothenberg had secured 59 per cent of the total votes and was declared the new president of the USSF. Fricker had relied on his track record being enough, resting on the laurels of winning the World Cup bid. The result was a vote for change; winning the bid in 1988 was one hell of an achievement but since then Fricker had appeared unable to push the process on. The USSF had been standing on the precipice with the member voters willing to risk it all with Rothenberg than the slow, staid approach of Fricker.

FIFA was elated with the news. Havelange and Blatter had seen Rothenberg work at close quarters during the 1984 Olympics and had already struck up a working relationship with him. Despite the Olympics being hosted by Los Angeles, due to its size, other venues across the USA were brought in to host events. A track record of contributing to a major cross-country sporting event was a highlight on Rothenberg's résumé. Due to the structure Fricker had created, Rothenberg became president of the USSF and chairman of the board for the World Cup. LeTellier remained head of the WCOC whilst many of the loyal volunteers who had worked tirelessly to get this far feared their journey was over.

'We didn't have a vote during the election but we were all present at the result in Orlando,' said Trecker, still at this point a key cog in the WCOC. 'Once the result was announced I turned to a colleague and said, "oh well, we had a good run while it lasted." We were what I called "Frickerites", I presumed Alan would want to bring his own people in.'

Trecker couldn't have been more wrong. Having done his due diligence, Rothenberg was only too aware of how vital the team at the WCOC were. They just needed to be put in the best position to succeed. 'Over the first several months, I knew I had to keep the people who were already involved,' Rothenberg said, 'but a lot more were needed.'

The scale of the job in hand was not lost on Rothenberg since the USSF was still primarily a charity organisation staffed by volunteers. 'It was difficult to step in, there was an awkward situation where the USSF and World Cup 94 were two separate entities,' Rothenberg explained. 'The USSF was still a grassroots organisation, there were things that needed to be straightened out. There was no pro league which had been promised, but to start one at that time would have been a huge mistake.'

Fricker's gameplan upon winning the bid was threefold. He had already dropped the ball in regard to the broadcast deal and the ability to attract large corporate sponsors. The final target was to get another professional league up and running. It was back in July 1988 when the federation signed off on Fricker's plans which he envisaged would begin the following year, yet 12 months on, nothing had happened. Rothenberg flew to Zürich and assured them that whilst a professional league was high on the agenda it would have to wait until after the World Cup, to which FIFA agreed.

One of Rothenberg's first moves was to demote LeTellier and replace him with fellow Los Angeles attorney Charles Cale, who became the chief executive officer for World Cup 1994 Incorporated. Another appointment saw one of the 1984 Olympic venue directors, Hank Steinbrecher, join the USSF as general secretary. Steinbrecher had been both a football player and a coach before landing the role of director of marketing for Gatorade which opened the doors to many of the top sporting organisations and athletes that the country had to offer.

Shortly after his appointment, Steinbrecher was called to a meeting with his new boss. 'Alan told me, "We've won but I don't know how to run a federation." My role was to prepare a football community to host a World Cup,' Steinbrecher explained. 'It was massively a volunteer organisation, we had to change the management culture, there was definitely an inferiority complex when it came to soccer, for too long we had been told what to do by others.'

During his time with Gatorade, Steinbrecher had looked on as the USSF floundered after securing the bid. 'I knew from other business people I had spoken to that they didn't think the USSF was capable of hosting the World Cup and they wouldn't commit sponsorship to it under that regime,' said Steinbrecher. 'There were only two sponsorships on the books when we came in, we had to infuse a corporate business style into a not-for-profit volunteer organisation.'

If the World Cup was to be a success, then first, they would need to increase the amount of money coming into the federation and the WCOC. 'I saw football as the USA's number one family game. We looked at the bottom of the pyramid, we had no choice because at that point there was no top. We contacted the state associations to register players with us and by doing this, we got 50 cents a name from FIFA,' Steinbrecher said. 'Through this, we developed a database of players which before then we didn't have, we could identify who was playing and where, which was invaluable as a pathway to the national team.'

The federation also needed to know what it was doing right and where it was going wrong. 'We organised a strategic summit and developed a business plan of how we could develop the game within the USA, we invited everyone we could think of to Chicago for the weekend, 250 people,' Steinbrecher explained. 'There were those who supported us and those who hated us but we needed to know what we needed to do to make football a success.'

The knock-on effect was evident, the USSF now had a database of players at all levels throughout the country. From this, they developed a mailing list of people to be used when the time came to sell tickets as well as statistical information to help attract the much-needed sponsorships which would fund the federation, the state associations and the WCOC. The marketing strategy also kicked into gear with the USSF rebranded as US Soccer complete with an all-new logo.

The snowball effect was in full motion, thanks to Steinbrecher's contacts and business links. 'We used the leverage of the World Cup to get them to also invest in US Soccer,' explained Steinbrecher. 'They couldn't have one without the other.' Sponsors multiplied from two to 24, raising the federation's budget from $3m to $13m.

There was another issue that the game's governing body was less than happy with. Rothenberg was president of US Soccer and so, in FIFA's eyes, also de facto head of the World Cup; after all that was what they had backed him to do. But due to the split organisations that honour had befallen Cale, who Rothenberg had installed to run the day-to-day World Cup operations whilst he resolved the federation's issues.

Cale had employed some new people to work within the WCOC and set up lavish offices at Century City in Los Angeles. He had also attended several meetings with FIFA as per the norm but then, out of the blue, Rothenberg was summoned to Zürich by football's top brass in November 1991. Upon his return, he immediately circulated a memorandum addressed to 'All World Cup 1994 Inc personnel'. In it Rothenberg outlined the plans for the World Cup going forward: 'To ensure that we realize our mission to present the best World Cup in history and leave a legacy for soccer in the United States and to better integrate the activities of the World Cup Organizing Committee and the United States Soccer Federation, effective immediately: Alan Rothenberg will be Chairman, President and Chief Executive of World Cup 1994 Inc.; Chuck Cale will be Vice-Chairman of World Cup 1994 Inc.' Alan Rothenberg was now the kingmaker of football in the USA.

The decision seemed a natural one as Rothenberg's suitability to the role of World Cup commander in chief was what attracted FIFA to him in the first place. He had a proven track record from his time as president of the Los Angeles Clippers NBA franchise through to his Olympics success. 'I went to the 1982 World Cup in Spain and saw how big an event the World Cup was,' Rothenberg said, who continued his usual practice of an 18- to 20-hour working day. 'It was exciting, I was used to working long days. I just did what needed to be done.'

To get around the lack of ad breaks, sponsors were brought on board with promises of their brand name or logo appearing next to the game clock for extended periods during the match. The result was emphatic, maximising profits with minimum disruption. With sponsors secured, the next major hurdle was selling tickets. Prices were announced, starting at $25 for group games with $475 the highest-priced ticket for the final. The narrative was that football wasn't for Americans, they just didn't 'get it' and had their own sports, but one thing they could be relied on for was supporting a major event. Except this wasn't just one event. 'When I tried to sell the World Cup to people, they often asked where it was,' said Trecker. 'I had to explain, it wasn't an "it", it's not a Super Bowl, it's 52 Super Bowls.'

Steinbrecher's groundwork with the state associations was about to be put to the test. He believed that they would be able to sell out all of the first-round games through the USA's football community alone. The WCOC marketing group weren't convinced but the results spoke for themselves. The football family came out in force, purchasing two million tickets in only two days. Only the fact that some tickets had to be held back for general sale meant they didn't sell out; it was later estimated that US Soccer could have sold 50–60 per cent more tickets.

'I knew these people were passionate about the game and they would be intrigued enough to buy tickets, it was a hard sell until the time came and they actually did,' said media guru Trecker. One man who shared Trecker's confidence was Rothenberg. With 50 days until opening day he told the *Los Angeles Times* he was confident that all of the games would sell out. 'It was partly salesmanship,' Rothenberg laughed. 'I was asked by a reporter if I had to hype it up as much as I did; probably not but I didn't want to take any chances.'

With tickets flying out, any pre-conceived concerns from FIFA had evaporated. Another clear sign of this was when, in December 1993, they reminded Rothenberg about the planned professional league which had been put on the backburner. 'FIFA had seen all of the work we had done with the World Cup so now they wanted the league starting,' Rothenberg explained. 'We had done no work, so now we were running the early plans for the league alongside finishing preparations for the World Cup. We created the business plan and planted the seed for what would become Major League Soccer.'

'I want to make clear that the World Cup was down to Werner Fricker, not me,' Rothenberg said, giving credit to the man who laid the groundwork.

'It was Werner's vision that got the World Cup,' said Trecker, who worked with both men. 'He wasn't the best man for keeping all of the plates spinning, that was Alan's speciality.'

There were six months before the opening day of the tournament and the hierarchy of US football had changed dramatically. The federation had come a long way from the days of Werner Fricker and his band of dedicated volunteers to the corporate machine it was now on the road to becoming.

Chapter Three

The Science of Grass

WHILST QUESTIONS were raised over the USA's suitability to host the World Cup from a footballing standpoint, one area in which they didn't fall short was its stadiums. The USA was full of them, in all shapes and sizes, from quaint baseball parks with green ivy-covered walls like Wrigley Field in Chicago, to the Michigan Stadium in Ann Arbor, known as 'the Big House', which held over 100,000 fans.

The sheer number of sports arenas in the US had been a huge selling point when FIFA considered holding the tournament there. This proved to be the case when US Soccer proudly announced that 31 stadiums across 27 cities had applied to host World Cup games, the most in the tournament's history. FIFA now began their inspection process, sending two teams to check that the stadiums complied with their standards.

Once the inspections were over and the reports filed, work began on whittling down the hopefuls into a final selection. 'There was initial hesitancy from the cities to come on board, some doubted that it would ever work,' said US Soccer president, Alan Rothenberg. An early idea was to use some of the smaller college sites around the country, but the US Soccer president had other ideas as he looked to utilise the vast bowls and arenas that the country had to offer. As the planning process snowballed and more companies got involved, so too did the cities who now had to pitch to the federation. 'They had to present what they could do, not just for the World Cup but also what football legacy it would leave in their city,' explained US Soccer secretary general, Hank Steinbrecher.

The USA was home to several huge domed stadiums, one of which was rumoured to be in the running to host the first ever indoor World Cup game. Houston's Astrodome looked doubtful as a venue since Texas was already likely to be represented by the Cotton Bowl in Dallas. The second indoor option was the Louisiana Superdome, but with the hurricane season beginning in the same month as the World Cup, New Orleans was also out of the running. That left the Pontiac Silverdome in Michigan as the clear favourite. The next puzzle was how to convert the artificial turf inside the dome to the natural grass surface that FIFA stipulated.

The Pontiac Silverdome was opened in 1975, cost $55m to build and was complete with fibreglass fabric roof held in place by air pressure alone. It was able to hold over 80,000 fans and was described by legendary boxing commentator Howard Cosell as being 'the finest edifice of its type known to mankind'. It was primarily home to the Detroit Lions NFL team but over its first two decades of use had also played host to Bruce Springsteen, WrestleMania III and Pope John Paul II. Now, if John 'Trey' Rogers and his team from Michigan State University could overcome the conundrum they faced, it would also be home to four World Cup games.

Trey Rogers was a 33-year-old assistant professor in turf management at Michigan State University when he stumbled across some of his more senior colleagues perusing a feasibility study. The report had been produced by famed agronomist James Beard and detailed whether natural grass could be used in an indoor sports setting. Rogers had already developed a keen interest in this having previously explored producing indoor turf for golf, but now the stakes were much higher. Football would certainly put the grass under more strain than the gentle pursuit of golf, but Rogers was intrigued and his more experienced workmates were only too happy to hand it over to their younger colleague when he expressed an interest in finding a way to keep grass alive indoors.

The very next day Rogers attended a meeting where ideas were drawn up; next they had to convince FIFA and US Soccer that Michigan was the place that could make it happen. FIFA's desire to host games under a roof continued and the Pontiac Silverdome was named as one of the nine host stadiums in March 1992. Now the real work began for lead scientist Rogers and his team. 'When the announcement was made, if I'm honest I wondered how we were going to pull this off,' Rogers remembered. 'There were 26 months to go and we looked at this as not only solving the problem for the World Cup but to also push forward the technology of sports turf going forward.'

During the first couple of months Rogers and his team repeatedly travelled from the university to the Silverdome to perform basic experiments, ferrying lights in and out to see how the soil and chosen turf would react. However, any progress Rogers felt was being made was being tempered by events that were out of his control. 'Every couple of months we would feel like we were getting somewhere when we would receive a phone call telling us to remove all of our equipment because Guns N' Roses were playing a concert there,' Rogers said.

Tom King was venue director at the Pontiac Silverdome and called the scientist in for a progress report. 'He asked me what my thoughts were on having a trial run,' Rogers said. 'I said "sure", we could have the pitch ready for April 94,' he continued. 'Tom told me he was thinking more like the summer of 1993 for the US Cup as FIFA were concerned that we weren't making enough progress.' Rogers and his team reluctantly agreed on the US Cup target but with the constant interruptions something had to give. 'I told Tom we would need a simulator dome built at the university which would eliminate lost travel time and help us avoid the events at the Silverdome.' In no time at all, the dome was erected at Michigan State University at a cost of $500,000. 'By this time, we were cutting through red tape like I would drink water,' Rogers laughed.

Having the dome allowed the team to figure out how they could keep the grass alive with minimal light, but due to the local climate any potential turf would have to be grown elsewhere. California was the chosen site which presented the issue of how the grass would be transported from one side of the country to the other. The initial idea was to store the materials in wooden boxes when a local company who provided equipment for the automobile industry made contact to offer their services. They would make dozens of hexagonal metal-framed boxes which would aid the transport, storage and installation of the pitch. These 'modules' revolutionised the process and once manufactured were lined up on the Silverdome car park ready for the turf, a combination of Kentucky bluegrass and perennial ryegrass, to be added.

Once primed, the turf traversed the country and was added to the modules atop six inches of soil, each hexagon now weighing in at 1.3 tonnes. It took the team 60 hours across five days to transfer the turf from the car park into the Silverdome but once inside, each module fit together perfectly, with Rogers amazed to discover there was no visible seam. A 2.25kg Clegg impact hammer pounded the turf to test its resistance and for Rogers and his team, the hard work was complete. FIFA had planned three more matches to be played after the US Cup game between England and Germany to replicate the four that would be happening the following year.

With the press expected at any moment, Rogers was asked when he would be marking the new Silverdome pitch out ready for the game. 'We weren't soccer guys so hadn't even thought of that, we had been so focused on getting the grass right we'd forgot all about painting the lines,' Rogers remembered with a smile. 'We managed to get someone to do it but due to the humidity in the dome we couldn't get the lines to dry. I acquired the help of my students who worked around the clock with leaf blowers trying to get the paint dried in time.' With the press throng keen to get a glimpse at the results of the team's hard work, the focus fell on the team of scientists. 'We had probably the first ever press conference for grass,' Rogers laughed.

The first game was a resounding success, German striker Jürgen Klinsmann in particular speaking highly of the pitch standard, much to the relief of Rogers who could barely bring himself to look when the German side took to the pitch for a pre-match warm-up. 'These are the reigning World Champions, I'm expecting them to pay close attention to the pitch, to be trying to kick the turf up as they are only used to the best,' said Rogers. 'Instead, the players gathered in the centre circle and started kicking the ball in the air as high as they could, trying to hit the roof. This was when it dawned on me, the pitch was nothing new for the players but playing indoors was, that was the novelty for them.'

The four games proved the science behind Rogers's methods. The grass had stood firm and the signs were good for the following summer when the eyes of the world would be on the Pontiac Silverdome. The modules were moved back to the car park and covered where they lay dormant over the autumn and winter. The grass went brown with sandbags deployed to keep out moisture as the harshest winter of the 20th century descended on Michigan.

As soon as spring had sprung Rogers went back to work helping to inject life back into the turf and by April the greenness had returned with the grass now much hardier due to its maturity. Rogers and his team set about transporting the modules from the car park back inside the dome with the crew able to knock 30 per cent off the previous year's installation time. On the weekend the pitch was installed it passed FIFA's roll test, which measured how well a football would move on the pitch. Incredibly it was up to World Cup standard when 24 hours previously it was stacked up in the car park outside.

The first test of phase two would be provided by the host nation, who faced Switzerland in Group A's opening game. With football fever growing in the USA, Rogers realised just how big a deal the World Cup was. 'A local TV network sent a camera crew down to watch us cut the grass, that was when I told my team that nothing would be off limits here. They were filming everything,' Rogers explained. 'We were fine with it though, we had nothing to hide and it provided great publicity for the area, the people, the stadium and the university.'

By the end of the four games the turf was ready to come up. It unsurprisingly showed slight signs of wear and tear. A local football club put the pitch to good use whilst the metal modules were sold off as scrap. The science was now in place. The 2002 World Cup saw a whole pitch move in from the car park on rollers whilst Tottenham Hotspur Stadium has interchangeable gridiron and football pitches. 'All of the advancements we now see all around the world stem from this,' Rogers explained. 'The Pontiac Silverdome was a precursor; it was proof that it could be done. A combination of science, a lot of hard work and flying by the seat of your pants. We had no blueprint.'

When it came to the other stadiums, one concern FIFA had was the distinct lack of an obvious venue in the New York area. 'This was the challenge when we took over, one option was the Yale Bowl [in Connecticut]. It was important to get a New York area venue,' said Rothenberg.

It was a sentiment seemingly shared by Sepp Blatter who expressed his concerns to George Vecsey of the *New York Times*: 'I know that he had been to the city a lot and he had friends there, maybe it was performance anxiety on his part,' Vecsey said. Blatter was widely expected to take over from Havelange when he stood down from the FIFA presidency and wanted to leave nothing to chance. 'It was Havelange who wanted the World Cup in the States, so maybe Blatter was genuinely nervous about it all,' Vecsey added.

The lack of a New York venue was good news for the 77,000 capacity Giants Stadium in neighbouring New Jersey. Despite its lack of natural grass, the former home of the New York Cosmos and location of Pelé's final game was chosen to hold seven World Cup matches. The stadium, also home to the NFL's New York Giants and Jets, ordered in some Californian-grown turf to seal the deal. For a World

Cup hellbent on holding games in the Big Apple, they had to settle for a short trip down the turnpike.

On the west coast, California was given two venues, Palo Alto's Stanford Stadium and the apple of FIFA's eye, Pasadena's Rose Bowl. Whilst all stadiums needed certain amounts of renovation to meet the strict criteria, Stanford underwent a year-long facelift with increased media facilities and the replacement of wooden benches in the stands. Texas was, as expected, represented by the ageing Cotton Bowl in Dallas, the city which would also house the World Cup's media centre.

Foxboro Stadium in Massachusetts was selected from the east coast while Orlando's Citrus Bowl beat out Miami's Joe Robbie Stadium, an early favourite, to be Florida's sole representative. The smallest of the nine venues, in close proximity to Disneyland, benefitted from Florida being awarded a new Major League Baseball franchise that would require the Joe Robbie Stadium all summer for their home games.

Elsewhere, Chicago's Soldier Field was selected for the opening ceremony and first game. The Windy City was also home to Soccer House, the new headquarters of US Soccer having been relocated from out west by Chicago native Steinbrecher. Washington DC was confident of being awarded games partly due to being the country's capital and partly due to their NFL team being in the market for a new stadium; owner Jack Kent Cooke was eager to have it host games. The plans went up in smoke when US Soccer dismissed his statement that any new stadium would be ready in time as fanciful. It was the dilapidated Robert F. Kennedy Stadium or bust for a city seemingly reticent to the round-ball game. However, under the guidance of executive vice president for the area's host committee, Emilio Pozzi, Washington turned into a football city, hosting two US Cup games in 1993 and five at the World Cup.

One of the largest numbers on the 1994 World Cup budget was for stadium security. With the expected huge attendances, the one thing US Soccer could not afford to have was a stadium problem. Despite not being in the age of global terrorism, the horrors of the 1972 Munich Olympics were still fresh in organisers' minds. San Francisco had also been shaken by the Northridge earthquake at the beginning of 1994; any repeat would have the World Cup hitting the headlines for all the wrong reasons.

Whilst the chances of another natural disaster were out of the organisers' hands, another potential area of concern came from the ugly side of football: hooliganism. Dubbed the 'English Disease', hooliganism had been rampant in both the domestic and European game throughout the 1980s. Rumours had it that England were purposely located in Sicily during Italia 90's group stages to keep their fans out of the country's mainland.

Now four years on, organisers believed that hooliganism's worst days were in the past, but Rothenberg still breathed a sigh of relief when England failed to qualify for USA 94. 'England qualifying was a concern whilst in Asia we could have also seen Iran, Iraq and North Korea all qualify,' Rothenberg remembered. None did though, and the bulk of the city and stadium security budget thankfully remained unspent as fans flocked to pack out venues as USA 94 transformed into a festival of football that the doubters never believed would happen.

Chapter Four

Arise America
before It's Too Late

THE 'SHOT heard around the world', as it came to be
known, secured the USA's qualification for Italia 90 and
with it legitimised FIFA's decision to choose them as the
next hosts of the World Cup. Paul Caligiuri's dipping 30-
yard volley was enough to beat Trinidad and Tobago in the
final qualifier but the performances that followed in Italy
showed just how much was still needed to be done on the
playing side. It was the USA's first World Cup appearance
since 1950, where an Eric Gaetjens goal shocked England
in their most famous victory to this point.

USSF head Werner Fricker planned to take a similar
approach to other American sports by installing a team
manager alongside a field coach. Talks had taken place
with German World Cup dual-winning player and manager
Franz Beckenbauer to step into the main role with Italia
90 coach Bob Gansler working under *Der Kaiser* until the
election defeat ultimately put an end to these plans.

'I was concerned after Italia 90 that we needed
professionalism at the coaching level,' Rothenberg said. 'I'm

not a soccer man but knew we needed to step up the coaching, Gansler was a great guy, American through and through but he was a college coach.' The search began to replace Gansler and after a shortlist was drawn up Steinbrecher was charged with interviewing the main candidates.

'The secretary general takes the suggestion of the manager to the president who then gets it ratified from the board,' Steinbrecher explained. 'There were many big names, Carlos Alberto Parreira, Sven-Göran Eriksson and Beckenbauer, but I needed someone who would come in, roll their sleeves up and get to work.'

Velibor 'Bora' Milutinović was something of an enigma. Born during World War II in German-occupied Bajina Bašta, situated in Yugoslavia's Serbian republic, his early childhood was far from happy. When the horrors of the conflict arrived at their door the younger Milutinovićes found themselves uprooted to live with their aunt some 30 miles away. His father died during the fighting whilst his mother passed away shortly after due to illness. The children were orphaned and, after leaving school at the age of 15, Bora and his siblings set off to Belgrade looking for a better way of life.

Brothers Miloš and Milodrad were unimpressed with Bora's apparent nonchalance to completing his schoolwork. Despite the elder duo being promising footballers, they were adamant their younger brother should complete his education. Bora's burgeoning skills developed and he soon superseded his brothers in the footballing stakes to the point where they relented and it became the family's singular focus.

Milutinović anchored the midfield at both youth and senior levels for two Belgrade clubs, OFK Beograd and Partizan, for over ten years. He also represented

Yugoslavia at the 1964 Olympics in Tokyo. Two years later the opportunity arose to move to Switzerland and for Milutinović there was no looking back; his footballing odyssey had begun. Over the next 45 years, he would play and coach in France, Nigeria, Jamaica and the Middle East to name but a few.

An obvious selling point to the USSF was the fact Milutinović had managed at the previous two World Cups. In 1986 he took hosts Mexico to the quarter-finals where they were defeated by eventual finalists West Germany on penalties. Milutinović had turned around Mexico's drab World Cup record whilst also securing their highest finish in the process. He spent the next four years in club football before an emergency call came in for him to coach Costa Rica, three months before they made their World Cup debut at Italia 90. Milutinović was a popular man of the people, could speak several languages and made friends wherever he went. During press conferences, he carefully trod the line between being open and cryptic, giving off the impression he was disorganised whilst also having a shrewd eye for detail.

Steinbrecher took an instant liking to him. 'Do not put this guy in a hen house, he is a wily fox,' he laughed. 'The first interview was in Mexico City and conducted in Spanish. As I don't speak it a translator was provided, now I knew Bora was a cagey guy and I was pretty certain he understood English.'

During the final meeting Steinbrecher set a humorous trap for Milutinović. 'Bora came to the States to finalise things and this time I provided the translator who I told not to translate what I said until I was finished speaking,' he said. 'I congratulated Bora on getting the job and said in English, "Now remember you must use the tactics and players that I tell you to." "No, no, no," he said, waving his arms. Bora, I got you! He was a genius coach, as he has proven in all of the countries he managed in.'

The appointment of Milutinović appeared out of left field, causing something of a furore amongst the federation with many having championed homegrown options only to see a non-American appointed. There was a method to US Soccer's apparent madness, however, thanks to the large Latino communities in the country. 'Hispanics love soccer and Bora was a cult figure in their eyes after the job he had done with Mexico. This wasn't the main reason [he was appointed] but something that definitely stood out,' explained Rothenberg. 'He had also worked at World Cups before, combined with his skill set he was an obvious choice.'

Milutinović's preparations with the hosts at Mexico 86 would stand him in good stead for what US Soccer had planned for the national team. 'Necessity is the mother of invention, our players were continually disrespected at international level,' said Rothenberg. 'Hardly any had professional contracts, so we had to figure out how to get players experience.' To begin with, the federation would build the team its own full-time training centre.

There were two locations in mind to be the squad's base, California and Florida. Mission Viejo had its advantages over Orlando: a temperate all-year-round climate and its proximity to Los Angeles, where eight World Cup games would be played. The decision seemed to tilt in the Californian city's favour when Milutinović moved his family to nearby Laguna Niguel. If the obvious kudos of hosting the national team seemed reward enough, the chosen city stood to make an estimated $4m in revenue whilst being able to convert the facility into another practical use once the national team had vacated.

USSF president Alan Rothenberg had settled on this decision from his headquarters in Chicago, noting that several other nations had a dedicated training base to work from. He had all too often seen players spend inordinate amounts of time on the road to games, practically living in hotels before heading back to their clubs and colleges spread all across the country. There was too much at stake for the national team; competitiveness and progression through the group stages was the minimum requirement.

The decision came on Thursday, 30 July 1992. Mission Viejo would play host to the USA squad and construction at the seven-acre Oso Viejo Community Park would begin immediately at a cost of $400,000 with an estimated completion date of spring 1993. There would be two full-size pitches, a training room, clubhouse and media facilities alongside a block of nearby apartments within walking distance. The city official promised a world-class training facility whilst the USSF guaranteed a £2,500 monthly allowance to the players who would be based there for 17 months.

One such player was Alexi Lalas who, having served his footballing apprenticeship at Rutgers University, had been part of the USA Olympic team at Barcelona in 1992. 'Bora had seen me play. I, along with a group of others, matriculated from that Olympic team to the full national team set-up in 1993 when residency started in Mission Viejo,' Lalas said. However, the promised world-class facilities had been hampered by an El Niño weather pattern that battered the Pacific coast.

'When we arrived in January 1993 the training centre wasn't complete due to weeks of massive rain,' Lalas continued. 'We spent a good month running on the beach in Laguna with limited field play. When we were finally able to train, the locker rooms weren't ready so a space was rented across the street in a strip mall. We changed opposite a Wienerschnitzel and next door to a Domino's Pizza restaurant. We then walked across a crowded La Paz Boulevard to the training fields. It was like playing US National Team Frogger.'

Once the training centre was complete preparations flew into full swing. Some players, such as Tony Meola and Marcelo Balboa, had experience from Italia 90, for others it was their first stop after completing college. 'I had been around the game all of my life,' midfielder Mike Sorber said. 'My father had spent 30 years as a junior coach, winning ten National Championships, and I had always played the game from parish teams in my St Louis neighbourhood to state games through to university.' It was whilst playing for St Louis University in November 1992 that Sorber's life would change. 'Bora was at the college championship to watch Claudio Reyna play for Virginia whilst I was lined up on the opposite side,' he said. 'After the game, I was invited to a training camp in December where I spent two weeks before returning to complete my senior year at college.'

With his senior year completed Sorber went straight to Mission Viejo at the turn of the year, one of five kept on from the training camp he had previously attended. There were 23 in camp with several first-team members unable to attend due to commitments at their professional clubs. There was plenty of work to be done, something Milutinović knew only too well, putting his players through their paces with twice-daily training sessions, five times a week. Weekends were different, with only one training session on a Saturday and the players given Sunday off.

'When it was finally open, the training facility was first-rate,' Lalas said. 'It basically provided us with a club environment. Some don't realise that when many of us stepped foot on the field in 1994 we had never been on the books of any professional club.'

The more experienced members like Balboa were chomping at the bit to be a part of another World Cup. 'At Italia 90 we didn't know how to prepare, it was our first major tournament. We were mainly a bunch of kids who had played at a youth World Cup going up against men,' Balboa said. 'We had been told we would physically match any side but when we lined up against Czechoslovakia, who had a team made up of players all six foot plus, reality hit.'

For those who remained from Italia 90, there would be a better understanding of what was to be expected and what level they would need to perform at. As he did with Mexico ahead of the 1986 World Cup, Milutinović arranged a heavy schedule of friendly fixtures with the CONCACAF Gold Cup and US Cup providing stiffer opposition as the tournament approached. The core of players based at Mission Viejo would be supplemented by European-based professionals like Caligiuri, John Harkes and Eric Wynalda who would rendezvous with the others for some of the warm-up games.

'The guys from Europe really added to the group in terms of ability and personality which dampened any resentment from the camp-based guys,' Lalas explained. There was no room for ego with players coming in and out at Mission Viejo's revolving doors, Milutinović leaving no stone unturned in finding his ideal squad for the tournament.

'We all had the same goal, whether based at Mission Viejo or in Europe,' Sorber said. 'We had no World Cup history and had gone 40 years between appearances. Everyone wanted to play in 1994.'

Signs that the training camp project was paying off came in the 1993 US Cup involving Brazil, England and reigning World Cup holders Germany. In a dry run for the main event, the hosts fell 2-0 to Brazil before invoking the spirit of Gaetjens to defeat England by the same score. German-speaking Thomas Dooley scored the first goal before the flame-haired Alexi Lalas introduced himself to the wider world by scoring the decisive second. The final game saw a narrow 4-3 defeat to Germany and whilst these results and performances had no bearing on the upcoming World Cup, it at least showed signs of progress.

The following month saw the USA progress to the final of the CONCACAF Gold Cup, where they looked to defend their maiden title from 1991. The healthy crowds from the US Cup couldn't be replicated as the attendances at the cavernous Cotton Bowl in Dallas were dwarfed by Mexico City's Estadio Azteca which acted as the second host city. The USA remained unbeaten throughout the group and knockout stage before the free-scoring Mexicans dropped a 4-0 scoreline on them in the final at a packed-out Estadio Azteca.

Milutinović, pleased with the progress, continued to work with the players at Mission Viejo with them now well settled into the residency programme. The players had become regular visitors to the local Ballpark Pizza Team restaurant whilst part-time musician Lalas brought his band to perform at Hennessey's Tavern in nearby Laguna Beach. The locals had also taken a huge interest in the squad. High-schoolers regularly clambered to the top of a hill overlooking the complex to catch a glimpse of the players training whilst the squad, in turn, staged football clinics for local boy and girl clubs.

The turnaround of players at Mission Viejo slowed as Milutinović zeroed in on naming his 22-man World Cup squad. The European-based professionals arrived at the training centre in May 1994 where they joined the residential players who had spent the best part of 17 months holed up there. The final squad was complete and before long they were on the move to the nearby hotel resort at Dana Point for final preparations before their first game in Group A against Switzerland, the World Cup's first ever indoor game. South Americans Colombia, pre-tournament favourites, were also in the group alongside a Gheorghe Hagi-led Romania who looked to build on their last-16 place at Italia 90.

With the double training sessions and numerous friendly games behind them, it was time for the USA to show what they could do. 'We felt pressure to do well because we knew it would reflect on the game in our country,' Lalas said. 'Getting out of the group was our goal. It meant validation, respect and relevancy amongst the game as well as battling for American hearts and minds.'

Milutinović, however, was dealt a blow when midfielder Claudio Reyna, fresh from turning down a move to Barcelona, was ruled out with a hamstring injury two days before the first game, paving the way for Mike Sorber to cement his place in the starting XI. 'From the 22 players I arrived at Mission Viejo with, five remained [at the end] and by the time the squad was named I was the only one left,' Sorber said.

On paper, the Switzerland game looked like the USA's best chance of gaining three points. The Swiss, however, had qualified well, taking three points from two games against Italy and boasted the likes of Alain Sutter and Stéphane Chapuisat in their ranks. The former had impressed with FC Nürnberg and would sign for Bayern Munich later that summer whilst Chapuisat was at Borussia Dortmund where he would win back-to-back Bundesliga titles and a

Champions League in his time there. His national team strike partner Adrian Knup missed the game through injury although manager Roy Hodgson welcomed back goalkeeper Marco Pascolo.

The crafty Milutinović had one last trick up his sleeve. The night before the game he took the squad to the Silverdome to give them a sense of what to expect the next day. As the players stood on the pitch gazing around at the mass expanse of the ten-acre site, the lights went off and a video put together by the coach played on the screen. Backed by a Van Halen song called 'Right Now' the video detailed the journey the squad had been on and in a sign of solidarity Milutinović ensured every member of the squad was featured.

As the sun rose on the second day of the tournament, the heat and humidity would yet again be a factor for the pre-noon kick-off, exacerbated by the fact the roofed Silverdome had no air conditioning. For the USA, reality was about to hit as the thousands of hours in preparation would finally be put to the test. 'It was a blur,' said Lalas. 'I remember walking on the field for the first time and realising there was no soundtrack. All my memories of spectacular sporting events had music and it was very jarring to not have that accompaniment. The Pontiac Silverdome was ten minutes from where I grew up in Michigan so to go full circle felt incredible. I wish I could have bottled that feeling.'

Any doubts over whether the home fans packed inside the stadium would know how to behave and react during a game were dismissed straightaway as chants reverberated around the Silverdome. Following an indifferent final set of friendly matches, Milutinović was adamant that his side would produce the goods when it mattered. Nerves were nowhere to be seen as they played the ball around, each team member eager for a touch with the defenders confidently starting moves from outside their own penalty area.

Captain Meola was soon called into action, scrambling across his goal as Chapuisat screwed an effort wide. An open first half ensued, both sides enjoying time on the ball albeit without the goalkeepers being unduly tested. With Wynalda and Tab Ramos hugging the touchlines, Stewart ploughed a lone furrow through the middle although chances were at a premium for the States. Switzerland, meanwhile, had experienced midfielder Georges Bregy pulling the strings, dropping deep to orchestrate play in what would be his final hurrah; the 36-year-old would retire after the tournament.

Dangerman Sutter broke through midfield where he skipped past Cle Kooiman before having his progress halted by a lunging Thomas Dooley. The German-born defensive midfielder appeared to play the ball but took Sutter out in the process. Argentinian referee Francisco Lamolina was unimpressed and awarded a free kick close to the USA penalty area. Meola lined up a five-man wall with both Bregy and Sutter standing over the wall. Bregy struck it; Meola having initially edged to his right side was rooted to the spot as the ball sailed to the opposite side and into the goal. Switzerland had the lead and what little air was left inside the Silverdome was sucked out.

With 45 minutes fast approaching on the stadium clock, Meola resisted the temptation to play the ball long and bowled it out as the USA pushed forward in the hope of creating a chance before half-time. Harkes strode forward with the ball, having only joined the squad 11 days earlier, the Derby County player burst through the opposition leaving Ciriaco Sforza little option but to bundle him over some 30 yards from goal.

Usual free-kick taker Reyna was still sidelined so the onus fell to either Ramos or Wynalda. The previous night, against Milutinović's wishes, Wynalda hit some free kicks eager to learn how the ball would carry in an indoor facility. This short bout of practice proved vital as players jostled to get involved in the set piece. 'I knew there was going to be a fight for it because everybody wants to hit free kicks,' Wynalda told SB Nation in 2014. 'I put the ball down and went into a zone. I really wanted to take advantage of what I had learned the night before.'

Wynalda stood over the ball. The California-born striker was struggling with an allergic reaction to a new energy drink the squad had been supplied with and felt fatigued having come out in irritating hives. With one swing of his right foot, he hauled his country back into the match. A sweet contact sent the ball curling and hooking over the six-man wall, with enough pace to send it arcing into the top-right corner of Pascolo's goal inching underneath the crossbar. The free kick couldn't have been any more perfect and with it, the stadium erupted.

The goal buoyed the Americans who enjoyed the better of the second half, looking much the more likely to add to the scoreline and seal all three points. As the minutes went by the heat and humidity became more and more of a factor; with both sides drained they seemed amenable to taking a point from the opening game. 'We were so dehydrated at full time,' Sorber recalled. 'I was called for a drug test along with Earnie Stewart. We had to wait two hours before we were able to give a sample, we were just downing bottle after bottle of water.' The hosts were off the mark however, already with more points on the board than they gained during the whole of Italia 90. With Colombia up next, the point looked vital as no one gave them a hope against the South Americans.

Pre-tournament misgivings about whether the American citizens would embrace the World Cup were long forgotten by this point as over 93,000 fans descended on the Rose Bowl for the second group game. The crowd was almost equally split, slightly leaning in Colombia's favour as a sea of yellow shirts took up large swathes of space in the stands. If the Silverdome had a claustrophobic feel the Rose Bowl was the opposite. Its roofless design allowed maximum sunlight with trees lining the view at the top of the bowl with a cloudless blue expanse above.

If previous records were anything to go by then the USA were heading for a defeat, having won only one of the eight total fixtures between the two nations. A good omen was that single victory came ten years previously in Los Angeles and lessons had been learnt from the Switzerland game. Colombia were a wounded animal having been comfortably beaten in their opening game by Romania, much to the shock of the pre-tournament tipsters. Almost immediately there seemed to be more support for Wynalda and Stewart in attack as the USA aimed to provide more of a threat whilst also keeping the door shut at the back with the hard-working pair of Balboa and Lalas.

The American front two had already caused problems before the troubled Óscar Córdoba in the Colombian goal continued his poor form by mis-playing a through ball, hiding his embarrassment by feigning injury following a Wynalda challenge. A pivotal moment came in the sixth minute when a Freddy Rincón cross caused chaos within the US backline who half-heartedly attempted to play an offside trap. Meola was beaten and a desperate Sorber could only reach the ball with his thigh, sending the Adidas Questra against the post then to the feet of Antony de Ávila. His shot caught Sorber's heel which slowed down the effort enough for Fernando Clavijo to hook the ball off the line as Balboa scrambled back to help. 'I just remember I had to get my leg up to the ball as someone was behind me to knock it in,' Sorber recalled. 'I got enough on it and luckily Fernando was on the line to clear.'

Both sides were lacking composure on the ball. Errant passes meant possession was changing quickly although Wynalda almost built on his wonder goal from the first game by firing a shot through a defender's legs and clipping the post with Córdoba beaten. American tails were up and just six minutes later they took the lead.

A ball to the left found Harkes, who ventured inside with Caligiuri overlapping with a lung-bursting run. With defenders having one eye on the rampaging full-back, Harkes swung a low cross towards Stewart at the back post. Defender Andrés Escobar lunged to snuff out the danger but could only divert the ball past a wrong-footed Córdoba standing prone in the Colombia goal. The USA were ahead with the first own goal of the World Cup; one that would have tragic ramifications for the Colombian centre-back.

With their future in the tournament hanging in the balance, Colombia coach Francisco Maturana made two changes at the break. However, it was the USA who started the second half stronger with Lalas hammering a shot in off the crossbar only to see the offside flag raised which, on replay, seemed unjust. The disappointment didn't last long. Following a patient build up, Wynalda found Ramos on the right wing, who played an exquisite chipped pass over the defence. Stewart used his pace to get in between Escobar and defensive partner Luis Perea before side-footing a shot past Córdoba that kissed the post on its way into the net. Stewart peeled away with a look of disbelief on his face before finding himself at the bottom of a pile of team-mates. Stars and Stripes flags were being waved with sheer abandon. It looked as though the footballing penny had finally dropped in the land of the free.

Going two goals behind did little for Colombia's urgency as they only seemed capable of playing in one gear. Ramos was proving to be a particular thorn in their side during the second half, bringing the best out of Córdoba on two occasions, once after a zigzagging run through the defence. Colombia had abandoned their earlier endeavours and reverted to type by attacking through the middle where their opponents rebuffed their advances.

The USA won a rare corner in the 80th minute. An outswinging ball from Ramos was met by an acrobatic scissor kick from defender Balboa. His effort rocketed inches past the post for what would have been one of the most memorable World Cup goals of all time, especially coming from a centre-half. 'It was something I practised as a kid,' said Balboa, whose Argentine immigrant father had played for the Chicago Mustangs in the 1960s. 'I tried one in the Switzerland game and many others before but not at that level, people were shocked to see it from an American defender.'

The home crowd were sensing the end was near when as one they stood to rally their team over the line. The cheers fell silent on 89 minutes when, following a strong one-handed save from Meola, Adolfo Valencia followed up Rincón's shot to put the Colombians on the scoresheet. It was nothing but a consolation goal though as referee Fabio Baldas blew the whistle shortly after to signal arguably the USA's biggest and most important win in their history.

Celebrations ensued with flags raining down from the stands as the triumphant players picked them up and took part in a lap of honour waving them above their heads. 'It dawned on me that we hadn't won a World Cup game since 1950. I looked up and the sea of yellow in the stands had changed to red, white and blue. Maybe they had those shirts on underneath just in case,' Sorber laughed. The Escobar own goal was already on Sorber's mind. 'It could so easily have been me but the post intervened,' he said looking back to his near own goal.

'It has since become a mythical game because of the subplot regarding Escobar,' Lalas ventured, 'but when we beat Colombia, we knew we had basically achieved our goal of getting out of the group. It was huge because of what they represented as one of the pre-tournament favourites. We had played Colombia multiple times so we weren't scared of them. The celebrations afterwards were pure American dreams. Holding up flags and celebrating not just a win for us but also for your country was magical and unforgettable.'

The USA had pulled off the shock of the tournament so far and found themselves joint top of the group alongside Switzerland with a place in the knockout stage all but confirmed. Suddenly the players' stature had been elevated: they had gone from unknowns at Mission Viejo to having their faces (and in certain cases hairstyles) splashed across the country. The USA backs a winner and, finally, their football team was just that. Group A's Jekyll-and-Hyde performers Romania were the final opponents, again at the Rose Bowl, as the USA chased what only two weeks prior seemed to be an unlikely top-place finish.

Hagi and co soon brought the Americans back down to earth amongst the thick Californian smog. The Romanians were patient and happy to pick the USA apart on the counter-attack with their attacking triumvirate of Hagi, Florin Răducioiu and Ilie Dumitrescu. A draw would have sufficed but the Americans had become thirsty for success after the Colombia win.

Romania had other ideas and hit the USA with a sucker punch after 17 minutes. Hagi released Dumitrescu down the left with a chipped pass and, anticipating a challenge from Balboa, the Steaua București man screwed the ball back to the edge of the 18-yard box. Răducioiu waited for full-back Dan Petrescu to run on the blind side of Caligiuri before playing him in. Meola, expecting the ball across the goal, left his near post exposed. Petrescu spotted this and slotted the ball into the gap the New Jersey native had left exposed.

It was a lead that the Romanians would not relinquish and, to add further salt to the wound, John Harkes received a soft yellow card for encroachment at a free kick and would be suspended for the next game. Suddenly the USA had gone from sure-fire guarantees for the knockout stage to now having to wait two days before their fate was decided.

'I think the Romania game was our best team performance,' Sorber said. 'Wynalda hit the post, we just couldn't score but I felt we got better with each game.' A win would have seen the USA top the group and stay in Pasadena where they would have faced a Maradona-less Argentina. Switzerland too had suffered an ignominious defeat after an impressive win in their previous game but due to a superior goal difference finished second in the group.

With the anxious wait over, the USA qualified as one of the four best third-placed sides and with it would make a short trip to Palo Alto's Stanford Stadium where three-time world champions Brazil awaited on 4 July, Independence Day. Despite the obvious uphill challenge that this presented, their initial target had been met. 'We had to get out of the group,' Balboa said. 'We had to succeed.

Everything fell into place against Colombia but we knew we had to play a perfect game against Brazil.'

Milutinović made two changes. One was enforced, Cobi Jones replacing the suspended Harkes on the left side of midfield. The other saw ten-year international veteran Hugo Pérez replace the opening-game hero Wynalda, who dropped to the bench. Milutinović had responded to the disappointment of the Romania defeat and recognised the importance of being able to handle the pressure of not only having the ball but also keeping and protecting it.

Whilst Brazil had not blown any of their opposition away up to this stage, they still possessed two of the tournament's most dangerous strikers in Romário and Bebeto. Both sides had played each other three times over the previous two years, Brazil taking the spoils in a friendly and at the US and Friendship Cups. Defenders Balboa and Lalas had yet to pit themselves against the 'Diabolical Duo' and they would pose a different threat to anything they had faced thus far. 'My challenge with Romário was his obvious skill, but more so his low centre of gravity and the ability to shift weight produced a quickness in his first few steps,' explained Lalas. 'As a taller player I was better matched up with the bigger strikers. I was up against it. Add to the fact he had the audacity and ability to score all types of goals, I just tried to limit the damage.'

'Soccer euphoria had taken over by the Brazil game, the nay-sayers and doubts had gone,' midfielder Sorber said. 'All of the negative publicity had disappeared; we had the whole of the country behind us.' The running track at Stanford Stadium kept fans at more than arms-length from the action but still chants of 'U-S-A' reverberated around the sun-drenched arena as French referee Joël Quiniou got proceedings underway.

A promising start for the hosts didn't last and soon Brazil had them under a sustained spell of pressure. A short-corner routine caught the US offside trap lacking and, similarly to the Colombia game, almost caused a goal, but defender Marcio Santos could only toe the ball wide of the goal. As the half-hour mark approached Bebeto showed how dangerous the Brazilian strike force could be with a scissor-kick effort that had Meola beaten, but that too sailed past the post.

Ramos was causing the Brazilians problems down the right, living up to his pre-game tag as the USA's danger man. His marker Leonardo, in a brief foray forward, had a shot comfortably saved by Meola but only a minute later the game was turned on its head. Ramos controlled the ball on the touchline with Leonardo in close pursuit. The USA number nine attempted to backheel the ball through the Brazilian's legs. Leonardo, sensing this, attempted to block it whilst both players' arms tangled. As the ball squirmed away Leonardo reared back and struck Ramos with a vicious elbow, the sickening blow sending the skilful midfielder to the ground with a thud.

Quiniou was immediately on the scene, brandishing a red card to Leonardo as the US players rushed to their stricken team-mate's aid. Taffarel protested the defender's innocence whilst Lalas argued back as the prone Ramos received treatment from the US medical staff. With worried fans and team-mates looking on, Ramos was carted away for further treatment whilst Leonardo was escorted off by pitchside officials. The USA played the remaining moments with ten men as Milutinović waited to see if there was any way Ramos would be able to make a miracle return.

The news was bad; Leonardo's elbow had fractured Ramos's skull and he was rushed to a nearby hospital. The half-time break flew by with US players eager to see if their team-mate would be okay as the severity of his injury became evident. Milutinović was equally as worried but also had to calm his players down enough so they could take his instructions on board as Wynalda replaced Ramos.

Despite being reduced to ten men, Brazil began the second half in very much the same way they had finished the first. Romário was clicking into gear, first beating Meola before Dooley could hook the ball away, the striker then having a goal ruled out for offside. The USA were increasingly unable to make the numerical advantage count. The ball wasn't sticking and no sooner had the defence taken a breath they were back under pressure.

The USA were now spent as an attacking force, their limited offensive forays had become extinct. On 73 minutes, Romário ran at the beleaguered defence before slotting Bebeto in down the right-hand side of the penalty area. Lalas, using every ounce of energy left in his body, threw himself towards the ball but Bebeto released a shot through the sliding defender's legs. Meola dived, hoping against hope that the ball would go wide. Alas it crept inside the post, knocking the water bottles over as it settled into the billowing, deep net.

Brazil had taken the lead and the USA didn't appear to have the time, energy or ingenuity to recover. Clavijo saw red with five minutes remaining, receiving a second yellow card for a block on Romário. The pocket-sized striker continued an infuriating Brazilian trait of miming a yellow card to Quiniou after the foul was committed. Brazil had out-shot the USA by 16 to four and the hosts' planned counter-attacking play had failed to materialise. The three-time winners had more experience and nous to not let the fact they had one man fewer for the entire second half prevent them from progressing.

As the full-time whistle blew the US players sank to their knees, their World Cup dream over. The fans remained, 84,147 had been in attendance that afternoon, and they stood to applaud a group of players who had contributed to the incredible journey football in the USA was making that summer. 'We were disappointed to be eliminated, you never prepare for defeat, almost two years of hard work at Mission Viejo was over in 90 minutes,' said Sorber, who would go on to be named the USA's most valuable player by Milutinović.

Looking back, the two defenders who had provided the bedrock for the USA's progress that summer had similar feelings. 'We opened people's eyes,' said Balboa who went on to play in Mexico after the tournament. 'Everyone still talks about the 1994 team despite us qualifying for the next two World Cups.'

As for Lalas, a spell in Serie A beckoned with Padova inking him to a two-year deal, but there was one man who he put his success down to. 'Bora changed my life,' he said. 'He wasn't right for all of the players, but he came at a perfect time for me. He forced me to think and that helped me improve. For all of his cosmopolitan experience, he had faith in the American footballer, he had faith in me.'

Football would never be the same in the country again and the faith that Milutinović had in American footballers spread as all the squad went on to forge professional careers in the game, many across Europe and Central America. A handwritten poster was displayed in the locker room at the Rose Bowl, on it were the words 'Four Points Then The Cup'. The team may have only achieved the first part of that statement but they had won over the US people, something that many deemed impossible just four weeks earlier.

Chapter Five

The Super Eagles Take Flight

AFRICA WAS viewed as the next great emerging power in world football and, buoyed by Cameroon's performance at Italia 90, FIFA allocated three qualification places from the Confederation of African Football (CAF) for the 1994 World Cup. Morocco were making their third World Cup appearance and Cameroon and their veteran star Roger Milla returned, but there was another African nation ready to burst on to the scene.

Dutchman Clemens Westerhof had been coaching in his home country for ten years when the call came. The Nigerian Football Federation (NFF) had turned to the Netherlands for a coach to take the Super Eagles to the next level with the Dutch way. *Totaalvoetbal*, as the concept was known, was still one that held sway in the late 1980s. 'I knew little of the country when I arrived and what I did know I had read from a book,' Westerhof explained.

His brief was to build a new national team that could primarily win the African Cup of Nations then go to the World Cup. His arrival was too late to impact qualification for Italia 90, although they still only missed out in the final game.

Despite being eager to steer clear of politics and concentrate solely on football, he reached out to the Nigerian government for assistance. Westerhof felt he had no choice: 'We needed to improve where we stayed, played, trained and ate, but we received no help at all.' On the pitch, however, Westerhof could see things were slowly knitting together. The ill-disciplined goalkeeper Peter Rufai had changed his ways whilst defender Stephen Keshi provided some defensive steel in front of him. There had also been some hierarchical changes at the NFF after Westerhof told them in no uncertain terms, 'Let me work, or I will go home.' The veiled threat worked and, with progress finally being made structurally, the search was underway for more players.

Westerhof flew to Port Harcourt to watch a young winger called Finidi George, who arrived on a bus with 21 other players. He was wowed by the future Ajax man and instantly invited him to national team training. Striker Rashidi Yekini was already part of the set-up and, when Westerhof saw him play in Portugal, he was taken aback by the pace of the Vitória Setúbal man. A tip-off from a fellow coach took Westerhof to Kaduna in the north-west of Nigeria. There was another player he just had to see.

Daniel Amokachi had been recruited by his local team, Ranchers Bees, at the age of 16 and within 12 months a besotted Westerhof had him involved with the senior national team at the 1990 African Cup of Nations. Westerhof wasn't the only one enamoured with the talents of this impressive teenager and soon Amokachi made the move to Europe with Belgium's Club Brugge.

Westerhof could see the perfect storm forming. 'It took one year but things were heading the right way,' he said. 'Everyone was on the same page. I felt I could build a team who would be unbeatable.' Two and a half years into his reign, Westerhof looked at the squad in front of him: Rufai in goal; Keshi alongside fellow defenders Uche Okechukwu, Augustine Eguavoen and Ben Iroha; in midfield, the technically gifted Sunday Oliseh, box-to-box workhorse Mutiu Adepoju, with wingers George and Samson Siasia supplying Yekini and Amokachi. Westerhof finally had the players, now he had to hone them into a team.

To be able to compete with the likes of Cameroon and Algeria, they would need more of Westerhof's two commandments: discipline and organisation. To begin with the Dutchman was unhappy with the fitness of his players: 'I told the NFF they were not ready for a World Cup yet but if they support me off the pitch then I will sort it out on the field.' Having sailed through the first round of CAF World Cup qualifiers, Nigeria were pitted against Algeria and the Ivory Coast in the final group stage where only the winner made USA 94.

The first game in Abidjan saw an early Yekini goal wiped out by a quickfire brace from the Ivory Coast. Two months later back on home soil, debutant Augustine 'Jay-Jay' Okocha gave the Super Eagles the lead before more goals by Yekini and Amokachi secured a 4-1 win over Algeria and the qualification dreams were back on track. When revenge on the Ivory Coast was exacted in the form of another 4-1 win, this time in the Lagos National Stadium, a point from the final game in Algeria would be enough. A tense affair in Algiers resulted in a 1-1 draw, Finidi George grabbing the goal which, due to Nigeria's superior goal difference, cemented their maiden World Cup place.

Buoyed by qualification, the Super Eagles took their form into the 1993 African Cup of Nations in Tunisia. They raced through the group stage before needing a penalty shoot-out to eliminate the Ivory Coast in the semi-finals. Zambia awaited in the final, still recovering from the tragic Gabon air disaster 12 months earlier which killed 20 players and coaches. A brace from Emmanuel Amunike ended the miraculous Zambian run and secured Nigeria's second Cup of Nations success.

Whilst fans of the Super Eagles eagerly anticipated the World Cup, further preparation was required, even after the Cup of Nations was won. Some quickfire friendly matches were arranged and three defeats to fellow World Cup qualifiers Colombia, Sweden and Romania were interspersed with a victory over Surinam. Thankfully, as fans gathered for the traditional tournament send-off game, Nigeria mustered a resounding 5-0 win over Georgia in Ibadan. Westerhof gave fans glimpses of future stars Nwankwo Kanu and Tijani Babangida although the 1994 World Cup would come too soon for them.

It had been five years since Westerhof had arrived in Lagos. Nigeria were now not only disciplined, organised and fit, but also African champions heading to their first World Cup and lay fifth in FIFA's world rankings. For the first time, an African nation boasted a squad of players who were all playing professionally outside of their own country.

They were unbeaten at home during this time and their manager was already predicting them as the surprise package of the tournament.

The draw put them in Group D alongside Argentina, Bulgaria and Greece and confidence was so high that they considered the 1986 winners as the only side that could cause them problems. Westerhof was happy with his squad. 'We had two players for each position,' he explained. 'I gave them belief, then watched them grow.' It was time for the Super Eagles to put this preparation into practice.

First up was Bulgaria at the Cotton Bowl, which had briefly played host to the Dallas Tornado in the doomed NASL back in the late 60s. The Nigeria squad had been welcomed to the Lone Star State by some from America's many Nigerian communities, backed by drums and traditional dancing. Despite being two of the lesser-known sides in the tournament, some 45,000 fans were in attendance for the evening kick-off thankful to have missed the Texan midday sun. Westerhof's preparation had not all gone to plan. Defender and captain Keshi was battling a knee injury and did not make the game so Rufai took over the armband in his place.

Although Bulgaria tested Nigeria early, the Super Eagles soon hit their stride. Amokachi had drifted out to the right wing where a hopeful bouncing pass found him in space, the Brugge man immediately brought the ball under control with his chest then teased the Bulgarian defence. The ploy worked; inside, George burst away from his marker and, with a flick of his left foot, Amokachi telegraphed the ball into his path.

George was clear in the right channel with one thought in mind: finding Yekini. Three Nigerian shirts arrived at the back post, the first was the rangy striker who steered George's pinpoint pass into the goal to give Nigeria the lead. Yekini's momentum took him into the goal where he gripped on to the net and let out a guttural roar. Nigeria had scored their first World Cup goal in a way indicative of their style and swagger. They had cut Bulgaria open with comparative ease and with 21 minutes gone had taken a lead they would not surrender.

Confidence soared throughout the Africans as Bulgaria failed to find a way past the in-form Rufai. Hopes were raised for the Europeans in the 37th minute when Eguavoen was adjudged to have fouled Bulgaria's star man Hristo Stoichkov. The Barcelona striker fired a 30-yard free kick past Rufai with his imperious left foot to seemingly level proceedings. Costa Rican referee Rodrigo Badilla raised his hand to rule it out, having initially signalled an indirect free kick, something that Stoichkov later revealed had not been made clear before his strike. This let-off appeared to wake Nigeria from their slumber and it wasn't long before they scored their second.

Two minutes before half-time, Yekini turned provider as Nigeria continued to enjoy space down the right-hand side. Bulgarian defender Tzanko Tzvetanov was dragged out of position and was unable to close down Yekini who withstood a hefty challenge before firing a low cross into the penalty area. Amokachi and Zlatko Yankov arrived at the ball simultaneously, the impact sent both players to the ground. With goalkeeper Boris Mikhailov in no man's land, Amokachi sprang to his feet and knocked the ball past the hesitant stopper. At full stretch, the striker wrapped his left boot around the ball and into the empty goal before falling on to his back. The Club Brugge man danced and Nigeria took a two-goal lead into the break on their World Cup debut.

Both sides remained unchanged as the second half got underway and within ten minutes of the restart the Super Eagles had put the game out of reach. Yekini's long legs took him clear of the Bulgarian defence as Mikhailov raced out and, with his reaction time severely reduced, the striker opted to shoot, his drive blocked by the advancing goalkeeper. However, before the defence could reset George looped a cross back into the area where Amunike arrived unmarked with a diving header to make it 3-0. Midfielder Adepoju was delighted with the perfect start: 'It was a huge morale booster. We knew how much football meant to our people and the satisfaction this result would have given to them back home.' The World Cup was on notice.

Bulgaria had more shots than Nigeria, but the Super Eagles were clinical when it mattered. Their three goals were not enough to see them top Group D, however, as a Diego Maradona-inspired Argentina lived up to their billing as pre-tournament favourites by demolishing an insipid Greece 4-0. *La Albiceleste* would provide Nigeria's biggest test and were up next at the Foxboro Stadium in four days' time.

Keshi was still absent and with left-back Iroha also out, Westerhof had to make use of the squad's depth as Michael Emenalo returned from injury to shore up the defence. Argentina provided a different challenge and boasted the likes of Diego Simeone, Fernando Redondo and Maradona in midfield. In front of them was the attacking triumvirate of Claudio Caniggia, Gabriel Batistuta and Abel Balbo, who all played their club football in Italy's Serie A, the strongest league in the world at the time.

In scenes reminiscent of the 1978 World Cup in Argentina the pitch was covered in ticker tape, the heat once again a factor with an earlier kick-off in Massachusetts ensuring more exposure to the punishing humidity. 'We trained in it so we were prepared to play,' said Westerhof. 'We had to train, no matter the weather. Sometimes the temperature hit 38°C, you just had to tell yourself it's not hot.'

Adepoju felt the players' backgrounds helped. 'Although we all played in Europe, we were African and used to playing in the heat,' he said. 'It didn't affect us as much as other teams.'

It was Caniggia who punished Nigeria with two quickfire goals in the first half that cancelled out Samson

Siasia's opener. A goalless second half gave Argentina the win and sole ownership of top spot in Group D. Westerhof was less than impressed with some of the Argentinian players' antics and the performance of Swedish referee Bo Karlsson. 'As we left the pitch, I asked him if he holidayed in Argentina,' he remarked. Lucky to escape punishment, Westerhof would have to regroup the squad ahead of the final group game with whipping boys Greece who suffered a 4-0 thumping at the hands of Bulgaria in Chicago.

Westerhof welcomed Keshi back for the final group game and, with Iroha still missing, Emenalo kept his place in the starting XI. Okocha was biding his time having made limited appearances from the bench up to this point whilst Yekini hadn't improved on his first goal against Bulgaria. The experienced Greeks appeared out of their depth and having boasted a side made up entirely of homegrown players they were looking to return home with something to show for their efforts.

Nigeria's best chance early on fell to George who, having played a neat one-two with Amunike, fired a crushing drive that rattled the bar of Christos Karkamanis's goal. Amokachi and Amunike also flashed efforts wide before the former was also denied by the Greek stopper as the first half appeared to be ending goalless.

With 45 minutes up and Scottish referee Leslie Mottram looking at his watch, Amunike broke from midfield. His massive strides left him desperately clinging on to his balance as he played the ball into the path of George. The winger knocked the ball down and, with a defender's challenge incoming, lofted a delicately chipped shot over the onrushing Karkamanis and into the goal to give Nigeria the lead. The goalscorer celebrated by dropping on to all fours and mimicked a dog relieving itself on the pitch, much to the amusement of his team-mates.

As the second half began the pace had slowed somewhat but soon news filtered through that the other group game (which kicked off simultaneously as was typical with the final round of games) remained goalless so another goal would cement Nigeria's place as winners of Group D. Early exchanges saw both teams trade shots with Rufai making a point-blank save. Amunike greedily shot whilst Amokachi and Yekini waited in the box; the Brugge man also hit the woodwork as the second goal remained out of reach.

With 49 minutes on the clock, Amokachi received the ball on to his right foot some 40 yards away from goal. He took off, evading a challenge as he brushed past four Greek defenders before arrowing a 25-yard bullet into the postage stamp of Karkamanis's goal. The Aris Salonika goalkeeper could only watch the net bulge as Amokachi scored his second memorable goal of the tournament. Bulgaria had shocked Argentina with two second-half goals leaving Nigeria top of their World Cup group at the first time of asking whilst also matching Cameroon's achievement from four years earlier.

Ahead of the round of 16 clash with Italy, Westerhof was dissatisfied with the squad's preparation. In his view the team hotel had become something of a magnet for hangers-on and the coach was keen to eliminate any distractions ahead of their biggest game yet. He planned to move hotels, something which was immediately shot down by players, unhappy at being uprooted at this stage in the competition. Rumours surfaced of players refusing to play should Westerhof get his way, the row was eventually defused and Nigeria stayed put.

Opponents Italy also had their problems. They arrived at Foxboro Stadium with the Italian press back home piling the pressure on coach Arrigo Sacchi whenever the opportunity presented itself. Westerhof's confidence had returned as he echoed Pelé's earlier sentiments by telling the American press that it was only a matter of time before an African nation would win the World Cup.

Okocha was named in the starting line-up, Westerhof was eager to get him on the ball and pick a way through an Italian defence that was missing captain Franco Baresi through injury. Ball retention would be key in the early-afternoon heat as Nigeria hoped to spring a surprise on the bookmakers' favourites. The plan didn't seem to be working, however, as Nigeria struggled during the first 20 minutes.

They won a corner five minutes later and George boomed a high curling ball into the area away from Italian goalkeeper Luca Marchegiani, who was deputising for the suspended Gianluca Pagliuca. Possibly unsighted, stand-in captain Paolo Maldini allowed the ball to ricochet off him in the six-yard box. Amunike pounced and with his left foot slotted the bouncing ball past Marchegiani to give the Super Eagles an improbable lead from their first attack.

Just as they had against Argentina, Nigeria had struck first, but a pivotal moment was just around the corner. A mere eight minutes after the Amunike goal, Amokachi was injured and unable to continue with the match. Westerhof changed tack and brought on midfielder Adepoju, changing the system that had got Nigeria to this point. 'The instruction was to have more presence and to control the midfield,' Adepoju said, explaining Westerhof's reasoning. 'We were already having problems but now we could take over the game from midfield and use our fast breaks in attack.'

The change appeared to have worked when Sacchi shuffled his pack, bringing Dino Baggio on for Nicola Berti in the midfield as the Italians desperately tried to find a way back into the game. Shortly after the hour mark Lazio striker Giuseppe Signori was also hooked and replaced by Parma's Gianfranco Zola, the diminutive forward who had learnt at the feet of Maradona at Napoli. To Sacchi's disbelief his move looked to have backfired 12 minutes after Zola's introduction when Italy were reduced to ten men.

Zola shimmied his way past Eguavoen only for the Nigerian defender to use his superior strength to ease him off the ball. With Mexican referee Arturo Brizio Carter well placed he quickly waved away Zola's protestations, who then in his anger lunged in across Eguavoen. The defender was poleaxed and although replays showed there was little contact despite the intent, Carter produced the red card, dismissing Zola and leaving Italy with even more of an uphill battle.

Buoyed by the numerical advantage, Nigeria attacked, Yekini muscled his way towards goal only to be unceremoniously dragged to the floor by the usually flawless Maldini. With cries for another red card, the covering Alessandro Costacurta saved his defensive partner and Italy from going down to nine men.

Time was running out for the *Azzurri* with the Italian press sharpening their knives for Sacchi with every passing moment. The usually cautious Italians were now throwing everything they had at Nigeria. Right-back Roberto Mussi raced down the line and, following a half-hearted challenge from Oliseh, knocked the ball inside to Roberto Baggio. Instantly *Il Divin Codino* rolled the ball into the far corner, just behind Eguavoen and out of the reach of

Rufai. With 88 minutes on the clock, the *Azzurri* were level and the game was headed to extra time.

The goal from Baggio demoralised the Nigerians and with ten minutes gone in the first period of extra time the Juventus man was at the centre of the action once again. Baggio received the ball on the corner of the 18-yard box and, spotting a run from Antonio Benarrivo, scooped a high ball into the area for the left-back to run on to. Eguavoen struggled to get ahead of him and clumsily fell into the back of the Italian, leaving Carter no option than to point to the penalty spot. Rufai fiddled with his gloves on the line as Baggio awaited the referee's whistle. When it came, he fired the penalty against Rufai's right post and in, the goalkeeper deceived and only able to fall to his left knee as the ball nestled behind him. A place in the quarter-finals had been two minutes away, but now Nigeria were 2-1 behind.

The Nigerian dream was over; despite what they had achieved there was a sense of regret and disappointment, a sign of just how far Nigeria had come. 'A huge festival awaited the players in Lagos upon their return,' said Westerhof, 'but I flew straight to Amsterdam.' The Dutchman had achieved what he set out to do, he had built a squad worthy of being ranked fifth in the world, but his work here was done.

The shock-and-awe style of play was a joy to behold and Westerhof appeared to have his team playing a style of football that was ahead of its time. 'It is common now because the concept has changed,' said Adepoju. 'Our strength was in transition from defence to attack and with our speed and power we were able to do that before the opponent could recover.' The more experienced Italians were never out of the game, even with ten men, but Adepoju was certain they were there for the taking. 'A second goal would have finished them off. We had the opportunity but ultimately we lost concentration and when they equalised it ended the game,' he said ruefully.

Nigeria would return to the World Cup four years later and whilst an African side would not fulfil Pelé's prophecy, the Super Eagles made history two years later, back on American soil. With Westerhof moving on, his assistant Jo Bonfrère led an exciting Nigerian side to compete against the likes of Argentina and Brazil at the 1996 Olympics in Atlanta. Buoyed by newcomers Taribo West and Celestine Babayaro, as well as Kanu and Babangida, the squad was much the richer for their travails in the USA. Against the odds Nigeria secured the gold medal, the first African nation to do so, a just reward for Nigeria's first 'Golden Generation'.

Chapter Six

From the Desert to DC

A MERE 50 years before the 1994 World Cup, football in Saudi Arabia wasn't even a 'thing'. The kingdom's religious beliefs and culture meant westernised sports were frowned upon, with the rules only being loosened shortly after the end of World War II. A national team was formed, although they would have to wait until 1970 to enjoy their first win, a 1-0 victory over Kuwait in the Arab Games. Dozens of clubs and pitches appeared across the desert as football took its grip on the kingdom.

Football had stormed the nation and King Fahd Bin Abdul Aziz was only too happy to fund the new pastime, using his vast wealth to cover the construction of a new national stadium in Riyadh that was named in his honour. The investments were paying off, Saudi Arabia had qualified for the 1984 Olympic Games, plus captured two Asian Cups at senior level. There was success at youth level too as Saudi Arabia won its second Asian Football Confederation Youth Cup in 1992, the first coming six years earlier in Bahrain. Subsequently this victory saw them qualify for the FIFA World Youth Championship a year later.

The progress was apparent although a World Cup place continually evaded the Green Falcons. By the winter of 1993, that was about to change. A two-week period saw a round-robin format of games involving Asia's big hitters. Iran, Iraq, North Korea, South Korea, Japan and Saudi Arabia would all slug it out for the two World Cup 94 qualifying spots that were available from the Asian qualifying section.

It was also only two and a half years since the culmination of the first Gulf War, when Saudi Arabia was on Saddam Hussein's hitlist after his forces invaded Kuwait. The fact that North Korea had recently threatened to nuke their southern neighbours only added to the organisational headache. Three of the potential qualifying teams, Iran, Iraq and North Korea, remained under sanction by the USA but any worries over their entry to the country were eased when President Bill Clinton assured FIFA there would be no such problems. Either way, a political dark cloud threatened the impending tournament.

All the final qualifying matches were to be held in Qatar's capital, Doha. Iraq, previous qualifiers at Mexico 86, stood in the way of Japan who were hoping to qualify for their maiden World Cup appearance. An injury-time equaliser from Jaffar Omran Salman broke the hearts of the Blue Samurai, however, and paved the way for South Korea who, having thrashed their northern neighbours, qualified as runners-up.

Another 90 minutes of drama saw Saudi Arabia vanquish Iran, 4-3. The Iranians twice pegged the Green Falcons back before Hamzah Idris appeared to seal the result for Saudi Arabia. A late Javed Manafi consolation goal made for several nervy final minutes at the Khalifa Stadium before the whistle was blown and the game was over. Saudi Arabia and South Korea had qualified for the 1994 World Cup, much to Alan Rothenberg and the organising committee's relief. A potential political minefield had been successfully side-stepped.

King Fahd's financial backing had brought success with the players reportedly each rewarded for their achievement with a car and 100,000 riyals. Qualification hadn't been without its ups and downs; coach José Cândido, and five of his assistants, resigned following meddling in team selections by the monarchy and was replaced by under-16s coach Mohammad Al-Khrashe for the remainder of qualifying. However, his permanent replacement was Dutchman Leo Beenhakker, who came with a more than impressive CV. Within months, however, fractures began to appear with rumours of clashes over tactics coming to the fore.

Beenhakker had managed his home nation at Italia 90 and knew all about the preparations required for tournament play. A difficult draw saw Saudi Arabia placed in Group C, alongside Belgium, Morocco and the Netherlands, one of the early favourites. With most of Saudi Arabia's games being held at the Robert F. Kennedy Stadium in Washington DC, Beenhakker recommended the Catonsville Community College just outside Baltimore as their training base, but then he was gone.

There were only three months until the tournament began and Saudi Arabia were again without a coach. With the exit of Beenhakker, King Fahd used his power and influence once more to secure Argentine coach Jorge Solari, after making a personal phone call to the country's president Carlos Menem. As was becoming evident, when it came to the national football team, whatever their chief financial backer King Fahd wanted, he got.

With the new coach in place, Saudi Arabia were the first nation to arrive in the USA ahead of the tournament. The team were now national heroes, dubbed the 'Brazilians of the Desert' by fans back in the Gulf state with veteran striker and star man, Majed Abdullah, christened the 'Arabian Jewel'.

As Abdullah's career was winding down it was widely anticipated that when the time came his position would be taken by young attacking prodigy Khaled Al-Rowaihi who had shot to fame when he starred in the 1989 U16 World Cup. These thoughts were dashed when the promising 20-year-old was tragically killed in a car crash in Jordan, 15 months before USA 94.

Creativity and a goal threat would come from the talismanic Sami Al-Jaber and the attacking Saeed Al-Owairan, although in qualifying it was the defence that had proved to be the foundation that Saudi Arabia's progress was built on. The retirement of defensive stalwart Saleh Nu'eimeh was a blow and suddenly their backline didn't seem as impregnable. Much responsibility now rested on the shoulders of 21-year-old goalkeeper Mohamed Al-Deayea, who had made his club debut five years earlier for Al-Tai FC.

Despite being considered as 500/1 long shots in some quarters, the squad were hoping to secure at least one victory at their first World Cup. The government too were eager to shake off the clichéd images of oil, sand and camels as they went on a charm offensive, hoping the tournament could also help to improve diplomatic relations for their country. Advertisements were placed in newspapers whilst brochures were handed out around the American capital detailing all that the kingdom had to offer, although there was a clash when tournament sponsors McDonald's used the country's sacred flag on one of its fast-food takeaway bags, a problem that had to be quashed.

Saudi Arabia's tournament finally got underway against the much-fancied Netherlands in front of a crowd of over 52,000 at RFK Stadium. 'We had played in the Gulf Cup, AFC Asian Cup and friendly matches against big name teams,' said striker Saeed Al-Owairan. 'The World Cup was something else, we were terrified ahead of the Netherlands match. There was talk of us being thrashed 12-0, but once the game kicked off we got it together and started playing with confidence.'

The Green Falcons stood out in their oversized, baggy white shirts, the arms of which dropped below the players' elbows. If the Dutch were hoping for an easy start to their World Cup campaign, they were in for an early surprise. With only one minute on the clock, a cross from Abdullah Al-Dosari was met by Majed Abdullah at the far post, his header creeping wide of the mark. Although clearly rattled by the Saudis' rampant start, the *Oranje* continued to play the kind of pass-heavy attacking football they had become renowned for. Al-Deayea stood firm in the Saudi goal as waves of orange were repelled, aided by a surprising show of profligacy from the Dutch attack.

The game's first goal arrived shortly before the 20-minute mark and it was the rank outsiders who scored it. A free kick from out wide on the right side was stroked into the penalty area by Fahad Al-Bishi, where midfielder Fuad Amin stretched to beat his marker and powerfully head the ball into the ground. The ball skidded off the turf squeezing between goalkeeper Ed de Goey and his near post. Saudi Arabia had a shock lead as Amin, a defensive midfielder by trade, wheeled away in celebration.

Going a goal down shook the Netherlands into life, suddenly their challenges had more bite and passes more purpose as they set about getting back into the game. Saudi

Arabia made it to half-time with the lead, leaving Dutch coach Dick Advocaat much to ponder. Whatever he said at the break had the desired effect as only five minutes after the restart they were level. Advocaat's side looked to stretch the play and pull the stoic Saudi defence out of shape but, for all their intricate play, it would be a howitzer from Wim Jonk that brought them level. The midfielder's 25-yard drive almost hit the same spot as Amin's first-half header, albeit glancing the post on the way in.

Advocaat replaced the ineffective Marc Overmars with Gaston Taument during the second half and he was quickest to react when Al-Deayea came marauding out of his goal aiming to punch a Frank de Boer cross. The young goalkeeper could only flail at the ball with his fist, missing it completely as he fell to the ground. Taument was free to head into an empty net to give the Netherlands the lead with only four minutes left to play, one they didn't relinquish much to the relief of Advocaat and their fans.

Saudi Arabia were defeated but far from disgraced; Solari cited the gulf in experience as the only difference between the two sides. 'It was an undeserved loss,' said a frustrated Al-Owairan, 'we did so well but came undone because of a defensive mistake.' In Group F's other game, played the previous day, Belgium had defeated Morocco 1-0 meaning both Low Country sides were joint top with three points each. A victory was vital for Saudi Arabia in their second group game with Morocco, a defeat for either side would surely result in an early exit from the competition.

An unheralded 72,404 fans were at Giants Stadium in New Jersey as Solari's men looked to build on their impressive tournament debut. In scenes akin to the first game the Green Falcons took another early lead, this time from the penalty spot when Al-Jaber dusted himself off after being felled in the area to beat Khalil Azmi from 12 yards after only eight minutes.

Eager to make up for his unforced error in the opener, Al-Deayea again kept numerous efforts at bay before a raking pass put the Saudi defence on the back foot. Great work from Ahmed Bahja down the left wing took out several defenders before he drew Al-Deayea from his goal and rolled the ball into the path of Mohammed Chaouch who made it 1-1 on 27 minutes. Unperturbed by the equaliser, first-game goalscorer Amin surged forward unchallenged on 45 minutes. Ignoring his team-mates, he hit a swerving shot from range which caught Azmi off guard in the Moroccan goal. Azmi was only able to palm the ball into the net as it dipped away from his outstretched left arm.

Saudi Arabia had won and were off the mark in Group F; Belgium's shock win over the Netherlands in Orlando had thrown the group wide open. Another victory in the final game back in Washington would seal a place in the knockout stages for Solari's men. They would have to do it without two-goal hero Fuad Amin since a second yellow card in as many games brought him a one-match suspension which saw him miss the Belgium game.

The pattern of the previous group games was repeated when the Saudis scored yet another first-half goal. Except this wasn't just any goal, this was one of the goals of the tournament. Only five minutes had gone when a Belgian attack broke down in Saudi territory, where the Green Falcons regained possession. Turning defence into attack, the ball was quickly played to striker Al-Owairan, who was still deep in his own half. 'I always enjoyed playing in the number 10 position, in the hole behind the strikers,' Al-Owairan remembered. 'I enjoyed the freedom that role gave me; I could drift into the left or right flanks.'

Quick as a flash he was away. His galloping strides kept the Belgians at bay, each time a challenge approached he touched the ball away keeping it under his control. 'When I first picked up the ball my intention was to pass, but the more I sprinted forward, the more space I found opening up in front of me,' Al-Owairan recalled. The Al-Shabab man took it past Dirk Medved, Michel de Wolf and finally turned inside Rudy Smidts as the Belgium goal came more and more into view. The last defender, Philippe Albert, and goalkeeper Michel Preud'homme desperately flung themselves at the ball. Al-Owairan, losing his balance, just did enough to send the ball between the two Belgians and into the goal.

The small section of Saudi fans roared their approval, as did the numerous members of the Saudi monarchy who had travelled to the USA to cheer on the national team. 'Credit goes to my team-mates, their movement off the ball contributed 50 per cent of that goal, it served me well and I took advantage,' Al-Owairan generously conceded. Belgium never recovered from the early setback and their attacks lacked vim and vigour. Saudi Arabia were more than a match for the Belgians and their second World Cup win left them and the Netherlands with identical records, although the Dutch won the head-to-head which sealed their place as Group F winners. Saudi Arabia were worthy runners-up and bid farewell to Washington as Sweden awaited in a last-16 match-up at the Cotton Bowl in Dallas.

The round of 16 match-up proved a step too far and the typical early goal this time would not be from a Saudi player, as Martin Dahlin headed home a Kennet Andersson cross to give the Swedes a one-goal lead. The tall striker went from provider to scorer shortly after half-time as his low shot beat Al-Deayea to put Saudi Arabia two goals behind. A sensational effort from substitute Fahad Al-Ghesheyan on 85 minutes gave the Green Falcons hope before Andersson's second just two minutes later extinguished any hopes of a late Saudi Arabia fightback.

For Saudi Arabia, the tournament was over, but they had provided plenty of standout moments during their four games. 'It was incredible, but we did feel that the Sweden match was the easiest of the lot,' said Al-Owairan. 'We felt we threw it away and were disappointed by the defeat.' Despite these regrets it was only the second time a team from the Asian Football Federation had qualified for the second round of a World Cup and Saudi Arabia would go on to appear at the next three tournaments without achieving the same feat as they did in the USA.

Al-Owairan received a welcome home fit for a king. Upon his arrival back to the Saudi capital of Riyadh he was enveloped by his new-found celebrity, King Fahd presented him with a luxury car as all and sundry wanted a piece of him. The goal against Belgium had elevated Al-Owairan's status astronomically and, with him already being a keen purveyor of the western-style nightlife the country had to offer, it wasn't long before his celebrity lifestyle caught up with him.

Within 18 months Al-Owairan was punished by his club for going AWOL for two weeks in Casablanca for which he received a fine and reprimand. It was early 1996, however, when he was allegedly caught by the police drinking during Ramadan with a group of acquaintances including some non-Saudi women. The authorities made an example of him and Al-Owairan was sentenced to a year in prison, the goal against Belgium becoming a millstone around his neck.

There would be a two-year absence from the national team for Al-Owairan as his team-mates won the Asian Cup in 1996 and secured qualification for the 1998 World Cup without him. 'The 1994 World Cup changed my life forever. I am still experiencing [the benefits] today and I will forever be grateful for that,' said Al-Owairan. Although they have failed to reach those heights again, at least on a global scale, during that one glorious summer the Green Falcons of Saudi Arabia left their mark on world football.

Chapter Seven

In the Heat of the Moment

WHEN JACK Charlton passed away in July 2020 at the age of 85 there was rightly a mass outpouring of love and remembrance for a man who dedicated most of his life to the beautiful game. At the 1966 World Cup, alongside brother Bobby, he was part of the triumphant England side who raised the Jules Rimet Trophy on home soil. Yet despite being a World Cup winner as a player he is more widely revered for the tournaments he led the Republic of Ireland to in the 1990s.

Charlton was born in Ashington, a coal mining town in Northumberland, a county in the north-east of England. He spent his entire 21-year playing career with Leeds United, the centre-half winning a league champions medal and amassing 35 England caps along the way. No sooner had his playing career ended, he moved into management first with Middlesbrough and Sheffield Wednesday, achieving promotions with both. Charlton returned to Ayresome Park to steer Middlesbrough away from relegation before two mixed years at their rivals Newcastle United. In December 1985, the Football Association of Ireland (FAI) approached Charlton to offer him the managerial post in the hope he could help the Republic step out of the shadow of their more successful northern neighbours and qualify for their first major tournament.

Upon taking over, Charlton decided that the quality of players from the League of Ireland would not be enough if they were to qualify for World Cups and European Championships. A memo was circulated around football league clubs enquiring whether any players would be interested in playing for the Republic of Ireland. They wouldn't necessarily have to have been born in the country but, if their parents or grandparents were, they would qualify through FIFA's Article 18, commonly known as the 'Granny Rule'.

This wasn't the first time that Ireland had used the 'Granny Rule' to their advantage. During the 1970s, managers Johnny Giles and Eoin Hand called upon the likes of Mark Lawrenson, Jim McDonagh, Gary Waddock and Chris Hughton, none of whom had been born on the Emerald Isle.

Faced with criticism from some quarters of the press, Charlton was adamant that if the country wanted success then they would have to have the best players possible at their disposal. Without them, Charlton felt, the Republic of Ireland would stay in the international footballing backwaters for good. The new manager galvanised the players and the results were instantaneous with the Republic of Ireland qualifying for their first European Championships in 1988. In Stuttgart, a Ray Houghton goal shocked England and Ireland exited having finished third in the group table, one place above the Three Lions.

Confidence was high and with more players coming into the fold, Ireland enjoyed their finest hour at Italia 90 when they made the quarter-finals of the competition only to be beaten by hosts Italy. A rare mistake from goalkeeper Pat 'Packie' Bonner allowed Salvatore Schillaci to give the *Azzurri* a lead they never relinquished. Nevertheless, the Ireland squad returned home to a hero's welcome.

Qualification for Euro 92 saw the Republic of Ireland grouped with England once more. Two disappointing draws with Poland cost Ireland vital points and eventually qualification as they finished in second place, one point behind England. It was a reality check of sorts and a sign to Charlton and fans of the Boys in Green that there was still plenty of room for improvement ahead of qualification for USA 94.

The Republic had now usurped the north as Ireland's premier team and were eager to prove this when both teams were placed in the same qualifying group. The Republic and Northern Ireland were due to face off in the final round of qualifying at the latter's Windsor Park ground in Belfast, a game that was sure to add to a pressure cooker environment that already existed off the pitch. Religious and political tensions had been high in Northern Ireland for many years during a three-decade period known as the Troubles. Clashes between Irish Republicans and Ulster Loyalists had resulted in the British military taking to the streets of Northern Ireland.

Qualification had gone well for Charlton's men and they approached the penultimate game with Spain knowing only one point was needed to seal a place at USA 94. However, a 3-1 defeat to the Spaniards set alarm bells ringing in the Republic camp ahead of the final game with their neighbours, which combined with the political issues only added to the pressure. Two days after the Spain defeat the violence that had become all too commonplace in Northern

Ireland reared its ugly head once more as a shooting triggered 25 more deaths in the next 18 days.

Due to the violence, rumours grew that the game would be moved from Windsor Park, with England and Italy mooted as potential venues, or at least have its kick-off time changed, a request immediately quashed as FIFA stated that the final round of games all had to kick off simultaneously. After much discussion, the plans were finalised. It would remain an eight o'clock kick-off at Windsor Park but with no away fans permitted.

The Republic squad headed to Belfast by air having been advised that road travel may not be safe. They arrived the day before the game, trained then waited to set off for the stadium. Accompanied by armed Special Branch agents the Ireland team bus made its way to Windsor Park, met en route by children with mock rifles made from sticks pretending to shoot at those on board. The players appeared under a cacophony of noise as police dogs took up position on the perimeter of the pitch. The first half saw little action and, following the break, word spread that Spain had taken the lead in the group's other major game, meaning if results stayed the same Charlton's team would be heading to the World Cup.

Shortly after the news circulated, the permutations changed. Northern Ireland striker Jimmy Quinn sent the home fans into rapture, giving his side the lead with a sumptuous volley. A response was needed so Charlton summoned Cascarino from the bench, only to find the lanky striker had left his shirt in the changing room. As Charlton berated the Chelsea man, midfielder Alan McLoughlin hit a volley of his own to bring the Republic level, sending a silent hush over Windsor Park.

The game ended 1-1 and thankfully free of trouble. The players left the pitch eager to hear how proceedings in Seville had ended. News filtered through. Spain, despite having been reduced to ten men, managed to hang on to their lead and both they and the Republic would be playing at USA 94. For Charlton's men, it was by the narrowest of margins: goals scored. John Sheridan's late consolation against Spain had proved to be a vital one. Hopes of peace had risen too; in between qualification and the start of the World Cup, a ceasefire was signed in Belfast.

Ireland were placed in what was widely regarded as a 'group of death' with Italy, amongst the tournament favourites, and Norway, who qualified ahead of England. Mexico made up Group E and were returning to the World Cup having been banned from Italia 90 for fielding ineligible players during qualification. They had finished as runners-up in the Copa América in 1993 and with the proximity of the host nation to their own were sure to be backed by a partisan crowd. This was an advantage that the Republic hoped to gain if they played in either New Jersey or Boston, where they were sure to be cheered on by the thousands of Irish Americans who lived there. The footballing gods answered these prayers by bestowing two group games at Giants Stadium in New Jersey, although the third would be held at the sweltering Citrus Bowl in Florida.

When it came to the squad, Charlton stuck with his tried and trusted options with many of the Irish players over 30, goalkeeper Bonner one of the oldest at 34. He had been a stalwart of the Ireland squad for 13 years but had found himself benched by his club Celtic towards the end of the season. Still, he was held in high esteem by the national fans, his heroics during the Romania penalty shoot-out at Italia 90 outweighing the mistake that sent them home.

The average age of the squad was reduced with the inclusion of youngsters Gary Kelly and Phil Babb, who joined a solid defensive unit that included Denis Irwin of Manchester United and Paul McGrath of Aston Villa, who had been shown the Old Trafford exit by Alex Ferguson but was voted PFA Players' Player of the Year in 1993. Kevin Moran added further experience in the heart of defence whilst the midfield engine room was manned by captain Andy Townsend and the brooding Cork-born Roy Keane.

The forward line provided Charlton with his biggest conundrum. First choice Niall Quinn had required knee surgery at the end of his club season with Manchester City. The 6ft 4in striker was desperate to return in time for the World Cup and, despite declaring himself fit, his club had other ideas and ruled him out. Fellow beanpole striker Tony Cascarino was another threat whilst Tranmere Rovers duo John Aldridge and Tommy Coyne provided further attacking options for Charlton.

Ireland arrived in Florida two weeks before the tournament began. Charlton was relaxed with his players, allowing them plenty of downtime so long as the work was put in when required. This was no holiday though as tensions ran high during one training session when Keane and assistant manager Maurice Setters clashed.

Charlton was away from camp at the time and Keane took exception to the amount of running Setters had the players doing in the debilitating heat. The furore raised was so much that a press conference was arranged to clear the air and for both parties to play down the extent of the incident. It was a foreboding of what was to come eight years later in Saipan when Keane was sent home from the World Cup for another bust-up with management after lambasting the preparations.

There were selection conundrums to solve before the opening match with Italy. McGrath was still hampered with a shoulder injury he had picked up the month before whilst Moran and Cascarino were also laid up with hamstring and calf injuries respectively. Charlton liked playing with a target man but with neither available he only had two strikers left in his 22-man squad. He opted for the erstwhile Coyne to start against Italy having been particularly impressed with his work rate since they had arrived in Florida.

Hordes of Ireland fans began arriving in New York. Tickets for the opening match were like gold dust with some changing hands for upwards of $250. There was a party atmosphere everywhere they went with thousands of fans lining the route to the ground, whilst bars in the likes of the Bronx, Queens and New Jersey were bedecked in Irish regalia.

Irish fans were buying tickets from anyone and everyone. As Giants Stadium filled up before kick-off the expected 50/50 split between the two nations' supporters was nowhere to be seen. In a stadium of 75,000 supporters, you would have been lucky to count more than 3,000 Italian fans. Officially allocated 8,000 tickets, the Irish had taken over with more than 30,000 in attendance making it a virtual home game for Jack's Army. Those who didn't make the trip stateside packed the pubs back home, apart from those in Dublin as the city's barmen and women planned a strike over work conditions on the day of the game. Whilst the Guinness pumps went into overdrive the length and breadth of the country, they remained off in the nation's capital.

Both Keane and McGrath passed late fitness tests to take up key positions in Charlton's starting XI. Everyone would need to be at their physical best as a 32°C heat would welcome the players despite a 4pm kick-off. The press speculated that the experienced Houghton would make way for the younger legs of Bolton Wanderers midfielder Jason

McAteer, but Charlton resisted and the slayer of England at Euro 88 took his place in midfield.

Any pre-match jitters the Irish team may have suffered were jolted when Dutch referee Mario van der Ende ordered them to change after they had donned the wrong kit. The mix-up was kept for posterity when the pre-match team photo only contained ten players as left-back Terry Phelan was still correcting his kit in the bowels of Giants Stadium. The disruption seemed to work in Ireland's favour as the hurried nature ahead of the kick-off allowed little time for nerves and, before the players knew it, van der Ende blew his whistle to start the game.

With only 11 minutes on the clock, Charlton's decision to start with Houghton paid dividends. Irwin played the ball inside to Sheridan who launched a direct pass forward into the Italian penalty area. It was met by Franco Baresi's head who uncharacteristically failed to deal with the raking ball from the Sheffield Wednesday man. Houghton tracked the ball's flight and intercepted Baresi's header, taking the ball on his chest as three Italian defenders gave chase. Steve Staunton overlapped to Houghton's left but the diminutive midfielder had only one thing on his mind. As the ball bounced, Houghton hit a 25-yard shot with his left foot that arced over the reach of Italian goalkeeper Gianluca Pagliuca on the edge of the six-yard box and into the goal.

Ireland had the lead. Pandemonium broke out in the stands as Houghton wheeled away, the 35-year-old inexplicably performing a forward roll before a disbelieving Phelan gripped him as Staunton and Keane arrived to join the celebrations. The shellshocked Italians took a while to recover their composure and find any kind of footing in the game. There were still 79 minutes remaining though and opportunities were sure to come.

Alan Rothenberg, US Soccer President and driving force behind the World Cup's success.

The Adidas
Questra, Official
Match Ball of
the 1994 World
Cup. The name
derived from an
ancient word
meaning 'the
quest for the
stars'.

Striker, the
World Cup Pup.
Designed by the
animation team
at Warner Bros,
the mascot was
a cartoon dog
dressed in red,
white and blue.

Soldier Field, Chicago. Host to the tournament's first game and its infamous opening ceremony.

Future US national team manager, Germany's Jürgen Klinsmann celebrates his opening goal against Bolivia.

The Pontiac Silverdome, host to the World Cup's first ever indoor game.

The late Rashidi Yekini, scorer of Nigeria's debut World Cup goal.

Diego Maradona rolls back the years for Argentina at his fourth World Cup.

After the own goal, Colombia's Andrés Escobar.

The hosts celebrate a famous win over pre-tournament favourites Colombia, at the Rose Bowl.

Mexico goalkeeper Jorge Campos brought his usual array of eye-catching attire to the world stage.

Saeed Al-Owairan, the Saudi Arabian attacker, scores one of the great World Cup goals against Belgium.

Republic of Ireland manager Jack Charlton urgently looks to get water to his players. The situation which saw him clash with FIFA.

As the dust settled on the Republic's lead, one thing Italy hadn't bargained for was the performance of Paul McGrath. Despite being hampered by his damaged left shoulder, his cool head and ability to read the game came to the fore. When Giuseppe Signori received the ball, eager to break through the Irish defence, McGrath recovered and at full stretch managed to remove the ball from his toe and send it back to Bonner. The Celtic stopper side-footed the ball out for a throw-in, a clear sign of his unease with FIFA's new back-pass rule. McGrath, in clear discomfort, stemmed the tide of Italian attacks as he put his body on the line time and again, first stopping a vicious shot from Roberto Baggio and then snuffing out a through ball from Demetrio Albertini.

Babb, making his competitive international debut, was gaining confidence playing alongside someone in such form, bravely heading away a Signori cross as the defence continued to stand firm. On the one occasion Signori managed to get away from McGrath he found his shot go wide of the mark. With the clock winding down the Republic gave everything as they worked tirelessly, hassling and hurrying their opponents. Substitute Daniele Massaro had joined Baggio up front but neither could find a way through and it was Ireland who came closest to scoring the second goal of the game. A Keane run and cut-back was dummied by Coyne before it found Sheridan. The midfielder leaned back slightly as his effort smacked against Pagliuca's crossbar with 15 minutes remaining.

As the seconds ticked away McGrath again stepped in, this time to block Massaro before winning a header from the resulting corner. Italy had channelled everything through Baggio but McGrath's performance was one for the ages. At the end of the game, it was calculated that he alone had prevented 21 goalscoring opportunities, all whilst being virtually unable to move his left arm.

It is widely regarded as the finest performance from a Republic of Ireland player, made all the more impressive when considering his injury and issues outside the game, battling depression, alcoholism and the end of his marriage. For 90 minutes, McGrath blocked everything out and ensured his country got three excellent points.

The full-time whistle brought further revelry from the stands as the Republic gave Italy their first opening-game World Cup defeat in 13 attempts. It was backs-to-the-wall at times, but Ireland had got off to a dream start much to the excitement of the fans who partied long into the New York night. As fans and journalists rang home to share their experience word came through of six deaths in County Down. Ulster Volunteer Force gunmen had attacked a Loughinisland pub whilst revellers watched the game. The atrocity proved that whilst the Irish were making friends around the world, much work was still to be done in their homeland.

During the flight back to Florida, Coyne was taken ill. Having spent three hours taking enough fluid on board to provide a urine test at the stadium he was now paying the price. The sheer amount he drank caused his kidneys to flood and the Tranmere striker spent the majority of the flight wrapped in blankets with ice packs on his head. Townsend was also struggling, waking the next morning with an alarming rash and swelling of his legs having suffered an allergic reaction to insect repellent.

Both players faced a race to be fit for the second group game with Mexico at Orlando's Citrus Bowl in six days. Cascarino was still struggling with his calf injury so the frazzled Coyne had become something of a focal point of the Irish attack, a willing runner who could occupy both opposition centre-halves. Charlton's fears over his players wilting in the heat of the Citrus Bowl saw one of several clashes with FIFA over the issue.

Before the tournament began a letter was sent to all competing nations explaining there would be a water break every 15 minutes with players able to have a drink in designated areas in front of the dugout. Charlton, already unhappy at what happened with Coyne, who was unable to shower or change during the wait for his urine sample after the Italy game, took FIFA to task.

With the mercury of the thermometer likely to be touching 38°C, Charlton questioned the rule stated in the letter. FIFA relented but President Sepp Blatter was rankled, saying of Charlton, 'He doesn't have a problem with water, he has a problem with officials at most stadiums and that is not FIFA's fault.' Whatever Charlton's problem, he may not have won the war, but he had certainly won this battle.

The pressure was on opponents Mexico who knew that another defeat would spell the end of their World Cup. They had already suffered a 1-0 defeat thanks to a late Kjetil Rekdal goal against Norway in the opening game as Egil Olsen's side looked to continue their impressive qualifying form. One thing that wouldn't phase *El Tri* was the conditions, whereas some Irish players resorted to wearing white caps during the national anthems. From manager Miguel Mejía Barón's starting XI, ten played their club football in their home country where June is one of its hottest months with an average temperature around 27°C.

A heat-resistant side full of quick skilful players was the last thing an ageing Irish side wanted to be up against in their second game, but at least the opening win had provided some breathing space. Barón rang the changes; striker Carlos

Hermosillo came in which pushed Atlético Madrid's tricky winger Luis García out to the left side. Ireland remained unchanged with both Townsend and Coyne able to shrug off their respective ailments to claim their starting places.

As the game got underway Mexico displayed the high level of energy and work rate normally associated with a Jack Charlton side. Ireland resorted to launching air raids on the Mexico goal with Bonner hitting balls up to the likes of Coyne, Townsend and Keane. Charlton later admitted the tactic was adopted to take some of the strain off players in the energy-sapping conditions.

The first half was one of little chances. Early in the second half, shortly after Townsend brought a save out of goalkeeper Jorge Campos, Mexico took the lead. García, Hermosillo and Alberto García Aspe all combined, with the former firing a low shot into the corner out of Bonner's reach. There were 44 minutes on the stadium clock and any notes Charlton may have made for half-time were now suddenly redundant.

Ireland regrouped at the interval, although chances were at a premium with a Sheridan effort failing to trouble Campos. Soon after the hour mark, García Aspe and García linked up again with the same result, the latter again beating Bonner low into the bottom corner. The second goal brought action on the Irish bench; Charlton looked to bring on his last remaining fit striker, Aldridge, with Coyne exiting having once again run himself to a standstill. Kitman Charlie O'Leary, however, had the substitute slip snatched from his hand by FIFA official Mustafa Fahmy. Aldridge was now in limbo and not allowed to take to the pitch.

The Republic were temporarily down to ten men, the spent Coyne had taken his place in the dugout, whilst Aldridge delivered an expletive-laden retort to Fahmy picked up by the touchline camera crew. Charlton's fury threatened to boil over and when Aldridge finally got on to the pitch Big Jack let the FIFA officials know his feelings in no uncertain terms.

The change had the desired effect as Aldridge flicked a header past Campos from fellow substitute McAteer's cross. The temperature had hit 48°C pitchside as Charlton charged members of his coaching staff and FAI officials with delivering water bags to his wilting players. A bewildered Houghton even received a yellow card from Swiss referee Kurt Röthlisberger for drinking from one.

As the full-time whistle blew the Irish players departed the pitch to seek refuge in the shade of the changing rooms. The previous day had seen Italy return to winning ways with a 1-0 victory over Norway which had left Group E wide open heading into the final round of games. All four teams had won and lost one, all sharing the same goal difference. Norway seemed most at risk due to having scored fewer goals than the other three teams. Aldridge's late header against Mexico appeared to be a vital goal.

The final game saw a return to the scene of Ireland's victory over Italy, Giants Stadium. Norway were making their first World Cup appearance in 56 years, their sparkling form throughout qualifying seeing them overcome both England and the Netherlands. However, it appeared to have deserted them with a narrow victory over Mexico and a disappointing performance and defeat against Italy.

The fallout from the Mexico game continued for Ireland with Charlton fined $15,000 and given a one-game suspension from the dugout for his outburst. He would have to content himself with watching the game from the broadcast booth high above the Meadowlands pitch. Aldridge's angry retort saw him receive a $1,500 fine but, much to Ireland's relief, no suspension. Experienced full-backs Irwin and Phelan were also suspended for the final group game having picked up two yellow cards in the previous matches.

Despite the Mexico defeat, Charlton was buoyed by the performance in the last half hour. Mexico had outplayed the Irish but, through sheer determination, they fought their way back into the game and almost forced an equaliser near the end. The problem now was whether Ireland should stick or twist for the Norway game as it looked like one point would be enough to get them into the knockout stages. A win could see them top the group and stay in New Jersey for the next round; however second place would mean a return to the greenhouse conditions of Orlando.

The Republic had gone unchanged for the first two group games but with the Mexico game taking its toll, changes were afoot. The suspended Irwin and Phelan were replaced by Kelly and Staunton, the Aston Villa man moved from a more advanced role into the left-back spot. His place was taken by McAteer, meaning the 'Three Amigos' of himself, Babb and Kelly were now in the side. Coyne enjoyed some respite of ploughing a lone furrow up front, replaced with Aldridge, who got the nod ahead of an almost fully fit Cascarino.

Charlton took his place in the stands, radio in hand, ready to relay any messages to Setters in the dugout below. Due to the group permutations and Ireland's new back four, Norway were expected to go on the attack. Shepherded by McGrath, the Republic would need to remain well organised with zero lapses in concentration.

Instead of the expected attacking onslaught from Olsen's side, Norway resorted to route-one tactics which were meat and drink for McGrath and company. The Republic, in turn, roared on by their impressive support once more, put on their most attacking display yet. Chances were few and far between, however, with Norway quickly running out of ideas and finding themselves resigned to their fate. The best chance fell to Keane whose chipped shot could only find the roof of Norwegian goalkeeper Erik Thorstvedt's net.

In keeping with the group's formbook, the other game between Italy and Mexico was also a draw, meaning all but Norway qualified for the knockout stages: Mexico as group winners, Ireland as runners-up thanks to their opening win, whilst Italy had to settle for one of the best third-placed spots. Ireland were through but they would have to play in Orlando once more, this time against the Netherlands the following week.

For the second consecutive World Cup the Republic of Ireland had made it through the group stages. The confident display against Norway had left many fans hopeful going into the game with the Netherlands, although not all shared in the positivity. Long-standing Irish football journalist Eamon Dunphy was a rare dissenting voice against the Republic, and especially its manager. He argued that Ireland weren't playing to the levels they should be with the players at their disposal and he laid the blame for this squarely at Charlton's door. With temperatures again expected to be sky-high in Orlando, the likelihood of the more pragmatic approach being utilised was a good one.

The argument that by playing this way allowed the players to gather their breath in the stifling conditions was countered by the energy it then took to regain possession. The Norway game had shown the Republic could play football, but would they be willing to go toe to toe with the technically proficient Dutch? Gary Kelly kept his place at right-back with Charlton looking to stop the rampaging runs of Dutch winger Marc Overmars. Coyne was back up front with Cascarino finally available off the bench if required.

The Dutch and Irish fans were two of the most popular groups in their respective host cities and had made friends wherever they went during the tournament. Over 60,000 were at the Citrus Bowl with many of the stands bedecked in orange and green. A potential quarter-final tie with Brazil in Dallas awaited the winners.

During the early exchanges, Ireland seemed determined to attack but it wasn't long before they were caught out by the Dutch. Overmars intercepted a poor defensive header from Phelan before outpacing Babb and squaring the ball for Dennis Bergkamp who couldn't miss. The Republic responded to going behind by attempting to put the Dutch on the back foot with counter-attacks, but their defence, expertly marshalled by captain Ronald Koeman, halted them time and again.

Any hopes Ireland may have had of a fellow northern European nation suffering in the dull but humid conditions of Florida failed to materialise and when Dutch midfielder Wim Jonk broke forward the Irish players couldn't get close enough to prevent him from firing a speculative effort from 30 yards. The ball went straight at Bonner but the experienced glovesman crucially allowed the ball through his fingers and into the goal. The Celtic stopper, in his 77th and final appearance for his country, slapped the ground in frustration.

It was 2-0 at half-time and Ireland found themselves in a similar position to the one they were in against Mexico. The Dutch were savvy though, pinning Kelly and Phelan back and taking control of all aspects of the game. Charlton threw on McAteer and Cascarino as they had no option but to chase the game, which wasn't one of the Republic's strengths. Cascarino gave Ireland the aerial threat they had severely lacked in games and McGrath saw a late effort ruled out for a foul.

The Republic of Ireland's World Cup adventure was over with the Netherlands good value for their 2-0 win. Charlton smiled as he left the pitch, proud of how far his team had come. Later, Dunphy again spoke out against the performance, firing another broadside at Charlton about 'unfulfilled potential' in his newspaper column. Yet the thousands of fans who had travelled up and down the length and breadth of the USA had enjoyed the time of their lives, so too had those back home who turned out in their droves at Dublin's Phoenix Park to welcome the team home.

Perhaps the Republic could have progressed further but the close-knit squad had just performed in three of the last four major tournaments, no mean feat for a nation of its size. The squad, a combination of old-school professionals and fresh-faced enthusiasm, lived and breathed the tournament. They enjoyed nights out with fans in New York and days at Orlando water parks, something completely alien to footballers of today. As was the Guinness tap that had been installed on their hotel floor.

Surly midfielder Keane later detailed in his autobiography that he felt Ireland's World Cup was over the minute they beat Italy. 'The World Cup ended that day in Giants Stadium. Beating Italy gave us a great opportunity to top our group and probably meet easier opposition in the second phase. Although people in our camp talked about the prospect, I think many believed that we were there to make up the numbers and avoid disgrace,' he said. 'Now that we weren't going to be disgraced, we could relax and party which was more or less the mood as we travelled back to

Florida.' However, the Manchester United captain would later play his words down by stating, 'Don't get me wrong, when we had to work, we worked.'

Team spirit could only get them so far, however, and whilst a game against Brazil in the quarter-finals would have whet the appetite of many, when combined with the constant battle with the elements, it would have probably been a game too far. The Jack Charlton era lasted another 18 months with him retiring in January 1996. There would be no further tournament qualification for the Republic until the 2002 World Cup, highlighting just what had been achieved during the decade Charlton was in charge.

When Charlton beat off Bob Paisley for the Republic of Ireland job in 1985, the FAI was in debt, Irish football was in decline and fans' apathy was exacerbated by the successes of their northern neighbours. During his spell, Charlton revitalised football in the country and inspired many generations to come. Despite his detractors, it is an era that lives long in the memory, made clear by the tributes following his death.

Chapter Eight

The Word is Freedom

THE END of the brutal Nicolae Ceauşescu regime in 1989 provided a rebirth for Romanian football. Having played in all three pre-war World Cups, their only other tournament appearance was at Mexico in 1970. The change into a democratic society had also seen home-based footballers allowed to seek fame and fortune abroad, something previously banned by the communist dictator. A generation of gifted players peaked together, benefitting from their new-found freedom.

Defender Dan Petrescu had found his form playing in the early 90s hotbed of world-class football, Serie A, where the dependable right-back plied his trade for Foggia and Genoa. Striker Florin Răducioiu had also made the move to Italy where he would play for four clubs between 1990 and 1994. Meanwhile, the hardworking pair of Ioan Lupescu and Gheorghe Popescu were gaining rave reviews in Germany and the Netherlands respectively. 'During the 1990 World Cup I signed my first professional contract outside of Romania with Bayer Leverkusen,' recalled Lupescu. 'It was a new start, a new chapter in my life and I had six wonderful years there. I found a manager who took care of a young player who made football my sole focus.' Lupescu helpfully spoke German having spent some of his formative years in Austria with his father, Nicolae, who joined Admira Wacker in 1972 having represented Romania at the 1970 World Cup. A smooth transition to playing football away from their homeland wasn't the case for everyone, however, as was seen with the one man who seemed destined for the very top, Romania's talismanic captain Gheorghe Hagi.

Once free of the shackles at home, Hagi seemed to suffer a crisis of confidence. During his childhood, Hagi had played football against his father's wishes and it was his grandfather, one of some 40,000 Aromanians who had arrived in Romania from Greece, who inspired a young Hagi's love of football. Despite his diminutive stature, Hagi was more than capable of outshining the older boys he played against, although his father took some persuading to allow him to continue playing, preferring his son to focus more on his studies.

Hagi started his professional career with Farul Constanța and soon his talents were recognised by more illustrious clubs. Hagi's time with Sportul Studențesc came to a controversial end when he was loaned to government club Steaua București ahead of a big game for the capital club. The supposed one-off arrangement was extended and Hagi ended up staying with the Romanian Army club, much to Sportul's chagrin.

Internationally, Romania stuttered out of the 1990 World Cup on penalties to Jack Charlton's underdog Irish side. Hagi's disappointing performances at Italia 90 raised suggestions that he would be unable to make the step up when taken away from the relative comfort of football in his homeland. Following his success at home and the ending of the communist regime, Hagi took the natural path to one of

Europe's big leagues by joining Spanish giants Real Madrid. He still carried the disappointment of Romania's exit upon his arrival in the Spanish capital and his early performances did little to dispel his critics.

Three meagre goals were all he had to show for his first season in the sacred shirt of *Los Blancos*. On a personal level, his second season was an improvement but an increase in his goal tally was overshadowed by a defeat to Tenerife which gifted the top-flight title to deadly rivals, Barcelona. The move had been a disaster and Hagi knew if he were to regain the swagger his swashbuckling style thrived on, he would have to set off for pastures new.

Over in Italy, Mircea Lucescu was forming his very own mini-Romania at Brescia. In 1992 he signed compatriots Florin Răducioiu and Ioan Sabău in a bid to sustain his newly promoted side as they arrived in Serie A as champions. The final piece of the puzzle saw him prise Hagi away from Madrid to complete a triumvirate of Romanians at the Lombardy club. Stepping out of the limelight did Hagi the power of good and soon his enigmatic gifts came to the fore. It wasn't enough to keep Brescia in Serie A, but he was back enjoying the game and unperturbed by relegation he stayed to help *I Biancazzurri* return to the top flight at the first time of asking.

Attention then turned to World Cup qualifiers, with Romania named as third seeds in a tricky group alongside the Representation of Czechs and Slovaks (RCS), Belgium, Wales, Cyprus and the Faroe Islands. New coach Cornel Dinu rang the changes with many of the experienced players from Italia 90 ousted whilst defender Miodrag Belodedici returned to the squad having defected to Yugoslavia three years earlier. During his time away the 27-year-old *libero* had added to his 1986 European Cup winner's medal by achieving the same feat with Red Star Belgrade in 1991.

Qualifying got off to a dream start as Romania put seven past the Faroe Islands followed by a 5-1 demolition of Terry Yorath's Wales. Ryan Giggs, who earnt his third cap as a second-half substitute, was merely an onlooker as a Hagi-inspired Romania thumped a Wales side who had beaten both West Germany and Brazil only months earlier. All five goals came in the first half bookended by goals from Hagi, his second an imperious drive from 25 yards out that Neville Southall could only help on its way into the goal.

Despite the thrashing in Bucharest, the return game in Cardiff saw the fate of both sides' World Cup qualification resting on the outcome. There had been a change within the Romanian set-up: manager Dinu was jettisoned after an embarrassing 5-2 defeat to RCS, who had also had two men sent off. His replacement for the final three group games was Anghel Iordănescu, who had served under Emerich Jenei when Steaua won the European Cup before taking the helm himself. He arrived as national coach fresh from leading the capital side to its first league title of the post-communist era.

Victories over Belgium and group whipping boys the Faroe Islands saw Romania arrive in Cardiff knowing that a draw would be enough to book their ticket to the USA. For Wales to make their first World Cup since 1958, a win by two or more goals would guarantee second place, whereas a victory alone would require other results to go their way. Whatever the permutations, Wales needed to win. For many of their ageing squad, this would be the final chance they would get to play at a World Cup.

Romania had the better of the early exchanges. Petrescu hit the post on 11 minutes whilst midfielder Ilie Dumitrescu wasted another chance seeing a shot sail over the bar. Hagi prodded and probed, drifting into space, picking the ball up and dictating play, seemingly at will. In scenes reminiscent of the first game in Bucharest, Hagi got on the ball some 25 yards from goal out on the right wing. As in Bucharest, he cut inside on to his strong left foot but on this occasion hit a low skidding shot towards Neville Southall's goal. The 35-year-old former binman dived too late, allowing the shot underneath him and into the net.

Further chances for Dumitrescu and Hagi were passed up early in the second half, something Wales capitalised on when Dean Saunders scrambled home an equaliser. Suddenly the game flipped, Romania looked shaken, and Welsh substitute Jeremy Goss's cross was miscontrolled by Gary Speed who fell to the ground having been ushered away by Petrescu. Referee Kurt Röthlisberger purposefully pointed to the spot and Romania were suddenly staring down the barrel of defeat. Prunea kissed the ball before handing it over to the Welsh full-back Paul Bodin, who placed it on the spot. With 27 minutes left to play, Bodin, normally reliable from 12 yards, smashed his effort against the bar and Romania were sparked back into life.

The pendulum swung once more, Romania regained their composure and, 20 minutes after the fateful miss, Răducioiu made Wales pay the ultimate price when he fired through the legs of Southall to make it 2-1. Romania's win saw them top the qualifying group. Whilst sealing their place in the finals by eliminating Wales, they also ensured there would be no Home Nations at a World Cup for the first time since 1950.

Qualification did much to lift the spirits of the Romanian people in a similar way that the Olympic successes of child gymnastics prodigy Nadia Comăneci previously had. They showed the world a view of the country other than that of poverty, disease and death. Upon returning from Cardiff, between two and three thousand fans waited at Bucharest airport in freezing conditions to welcome their heroes home.

The national team was a source of great pride for the downtrodden people of Romania, some of whom would travel to away qualifiers just so they could seek asylum in the opponents' countries. From the 300 fans who made the trip to Belgium in 1992, only 150 returned, such was the hardship they were experiencing at home. World Cup qualification was a sign of hope and an impact on many facets of life both economically and spiritually.

Romania arrived in the USA much different from the squad who faltered in Italy four years earlier. The draw had been unkind with Romania placed in Group A with the hosts USA, fellow Europeans Switzerland and pre-tournament favourites, Colombia. Romania were quietly confident, however, as the counter-attacking style Iordănescu had developed was perfect for this group of players. They were also battle-hardened with the experience of playing overseas exposing them to a new way of life, culture and different playing styles.

'We brought our experiences from the different leagues back to the national team, we created a good group with an incredible spirit combined with a winning mentality,' stated Lupescu. 'The most important lesson we had learned from Italia 90 was that we realised the "big teams" are not better than us, so we lost any inferiority complex we had.'

Over 91,000 fans packed into the Rose Bowl to catch a glimpse of one of the pre-tournament favourites Colombia. For Romania, Iordănescu fielded seven players who played their club football around Europe whilst the city of Bucharest was represented with the remaining four in the starting XI coming from Rapid, Dinamo and Steaua. The goal threat came from Răducioiu who had left Brescia for AC Milan and Dumitrescu who would finally leave Romania at the tournament's end to forge a career in England.

The prickly Hagi had been singled out for special attention by the football press, much to his irritation, as they talked up the clash between him and Colombia's equivalent playmaker, the unmistakable Carlos Valderrama. The flamboyant Colombian captain was the polar opposite of Hagi and seemed to enjoy the press attention and expectations that came with it. Hagi, on the other hand, was eager to exorcise the demons of his first World Cup but, in order to do this, he would have to keep his temper in check. A pre-tournament friendly with Northern Ireland had seen him sent off for spitting in an opponent's face.

Perhaps all the pre-tournament fawning had a negative effect on the Colombians but either way Iordănescu's tried and trusted game plan pulled their South American opponents apart. 'We knew we had a good team, but when you play in front of 90,000 Colombians in the first match your legs start to shake,' laughed Lupescu. Although Colombia did have their chances and were more than purposeful in attack, each time they found Bogdan Stelea in the Romanian goal more than a match for them. Romania's confidence grew as Colombia's aggressive attacking nature played straight into their hands and with only 15 minutes on the clock, the deadlock was broken.

Romania transitioned from defence to attack with ease, the ball found Hagi in the centre circle who performed a deft dummy to take out his marker. Răducioiu tore off ahead with four Colombian defenders scrambling back awaiting Hagi's next move. He fed a pass through to Răducioiu who had taken up a position in the left channel, his first touch wrong-footed the defence and brought the ball inside on to his preferred right foot. With more attacking options racing to join him, the striker angled a shot across Óscar Córdoba in the Colombian goal and into the far corner.

The predominantly Colombian-supporting crowd fell silent. A mere 3,200 Romanians had purchased tickets, but it was unclear how many had actually travelled with the US immigration service less than keen to issue visas knowing the reputation of the travelling fans. Colombia rallied with Freddy Rincón who was unlucky not to bring his side level on 23 minutes; Stelea stood firm once more, this time from point-blank range having moments earlier tipped a shot around the post.

Buoyed by his part in the first goal, Hagi was growing in confidence and knowing the habit Colombian goalkeepers had for straying off their line, attempted to lob Córdoba from some 35 yards. The man called on to replace the erratic René Higuita between the sticks somehow managed to get a fingertip to the ball and guide it wide of the goal. This warning from Hagi was not heeded and minutes later Córdoba was caught out once more. Dorinel Munteanu took up Hagi's usual position as the gifted playmaker drifted out to the left wing. Munteanu played the ball wide and continued his run. Hagi, ten yards in from the touchline, saw Córdoba again some distance from his line and with his wand-like left foot sent a swerving shot arrowing over the goalkeeper and into the far corner. It was 2-0 and Colombia's World Cup hopes looked to be in tatters.

As with any 2-0 scoreline, the next goal was vital. Shortly before half-time it was Colombia who got themselves back into the match with an Adolfo Valencia header, taking advantage of Romania being temporarily reduced to ten men with Hagi off the pitch receiving treatment following a heavy Gabriel Gómez challenge. It was 2-1 at half-time with the match now seemingly back in the balance.

Hagi was in the middle of everything but the pre-match hype behind the battle of the number tens had failed to materialise with the game passing Valderrama by. Colombian striker Faustino Asprilla was being expertly marshalled by Daniel Prodan and restricted to half-chances only. The diminutive Hagi was in his element pulling the strings, alternating between conserving energy and controlling play. Once the ball was in his possession it was near impossible for the Colombians to regain it.

With two minutes remaining, Hagi caught the Colombians sleeping and whipped a quick free kick into Răducioiu's path, his touch took the ball past the ever-onrushing Córdoba before he slotted it home to make the scoreline 3-1. A dumbfounded Colombia coach, Francisco Maturana, told the press after the game that, 'They let us have the ball,' emphasising Romania's comfort in allowing Colombia to play. The 1994 World Cup had a new set of dark horses.

Victory in the second game would see Romania be the first team to qualify for the knockout stages. Switzerland were no pushovers, however, and were eager for their first three points having played out a 1-1 draw in their opening match with the hosts at the indoor Pontiac Silverdome. This experience stood the Swiss in good stead; blond-maned attacker Alain Sutter had already seen a goal disallowed before he broke the deadlock after 15 minutes. Dumitrescu could only clear a Christopher Ohrel cross as far as the FC Nürnberg man who despatched it with aplomb. The same tactics employed in the Colombia game were not working for Romania here and other than two Popescu half-chances the *Tricolorii* had little to show for their efforts. With 35 minutes gone all that changed when Hagi stepped up to bring his side level, smashing a 25-yard effort low past Swiss goalkeeper Marco Pascolo for his second goal of the tournament.

The second half was all Switzerland. Romania were again punished for failing to clear danger and despite a hint of handball, Stephane Chapuisat slotted home after a scramble in the six-yard box. Swiss tails were up and Hagi had been reduced to a watching brief. Ciriaco Sforza broke down the right side and played in striker Adrian Knup who rolled the ball into the net for Switzerland's third. Seven minutes later Knup helped himself to his second with a header from a Georges Bregy free kick. To compound Romania's misery substitute Ioan Vladiou was sent off for a lunge on Ohrel only minutes after coming on. Romania were soundly beaten and looked a shadow of the side who had put Colombia to the sword in the opening game.

There was a reaction from Iordănescu ahead of the vital USA game. Firstly, the red-carded Vladiou was sent home following further disciplinary issues and goalkeeper Stelea was replaced by Florin Prunea, his heroics in the Colombia game quickly forgotten after the Swiss debacle. Tibor Selymes came into the defence in place of Dinamo Bucureşti's Gheorghe Mihali. Lupescu put the defeat down to one thing: 'Our over confidence was the reason we lost but it made us realise how important it is to be humble, concentrated and focused on the next match.'

It was back to the heat of Pasadena's Rose Bowl for the USA game, where another crowd north of 90,000 hoped to see a second victory for the buoyant hosts. Temperatures pitchside hit 46°C as Romania adjusted their usual counter-attacking style. Iordănescu packed the defence in the energy-sapping conditions knowing that a point would be enough to see them through to the knockout stages. Romania were not helped by some less than favourable kick-off times. 'They were a disaster,' recalled Lupescu. 'We had 1pm kick off times in 40–42°C heat, but even the evening kick-offs were 28°C!'

In sharp contrast to the approach Colombia took in the previous game, Romania attacked the USA down both flanks, testing goalkeeper Tony Meola with crosses from either side. This approach paid dividends; Răducioiu slid a pass inside the USA defence where the overlapping Petrescu ran on to the feed. With Meola edging away from his line expecting a cross, the full-back slotted the ball between the goalkeeper and his near post. It was a goal that smacked of naivety on the hosts' part and savvy know-how from Petrescu, who would swap Italy for England at the tournament's end.

Meola's mistake left him rattled with the stopper fumbling two basic efforts before the end of the first half. The *Tricolorii* defence had stood firm, a plethora of corners for the Americans came to nought and their lack of attacking ingenuity meant Romania had topped Group A. For the second successive World Cup Romania had advanced to the knockout stages where they would return to the Rose Bowl to meet Argentina in the second round.

Both sides previously met at Italia 90 where they played out a 1-1 draw. However the ban issued to Argentina's captain meant there would be no repeat of Hagi and Diego Maradona going toe to toe. 'We had previous experience of Maradona from Italia 90,' said Lupescu. 'He was a great player and we hoped that he would play, with him or not we would have played in the same way.' Also missing for Argentina was the injured striker Claudio Caniggia, whilst Iordănescu had a problem of his own, having to replace the suspended Răducioiu. He decided to push Dumitrescu forward and pack the midfield making Romania hard to break down whilst also equally equipped to attack.

The early exchanges gave no hint that this would be the widely anticipated game of the tournament. Romania sat back, solid in their shape, whilst Argentina, with Ariel Ortega employed in Maradona's role, stroked the ball about at will. With Caniggia out, Argentina coach Alfio Basile would be banking on Gabriel Batistuta and Abel Balbo as his main threats. It was Balbo who created the first chance: midfield general Diego Simeone played him in with only Stelea to beat, but the Roma man hesitated long enough for the keeper to pounce at his feet.

They would live to rue the miss as moments later Romania took the lead from a free kick in a position not too dissimilar to where Hagi beat Córdoba in the opening game. This time, however, it was Dumitrescu and not Hagi stood over the ball with a three-man wall attempting to block his path. He stepped up and curled the ball with his right foot, high over everyone and into the top corner, leaving goalkeeper Luis Islas flailing at thin air. The goal had come against the run of play but Romania had the lead.

Romania weren't ahead for long, though. Ortega played Batistuta in on the left-hand side of the box, outnumbered and with seemingly nowhere to go. Facing away from goal Batistuta backheeled the ball past Daniel Prodan whose slight lean was enough to send the Argentine striker tumbling to the floor. Referee Pierluigi Pairetto from Italy pointed to the spot and *Batigol* fired home the subsequent penalty to rub salt into the wound. With 15 minutes gone the game was all square again.

Hagi was beginning to weave his magic, roaming all over the pitch. Iordănescu's choice to overload the midfield gave Hagi free licence, finding pockets of space knowing there was adequate cover behind him. Three minutes after the controversial penalty, Romania were ahead once more. In typical style, Romania won the ball back and raced into attack. Petrescu released Hagi on the right side who played an exquisite one-two with Lupescu. Having received the ball back, Hagi delayed and with Fernando Cáceres unsure of whether to challenge or not, he weighted a beautiful pass through three defenders to the onrushing Dumitrescu who cushioned it past Islas and into the goal. Romania had again scored one of the goals of the tournament and were back in front.

Despite Ortega's selection it seemed that Fernando Redondo had taken it upon himself to fill any Maradona-shaped hole in the Argentina side. Early in the second half he had a good shout for a penalty and was increasingly stamping his influence on the game. One thing Argentina couldn't account for was Romania's ability to break at will, despite the ever-present brutal temperatures.

Dumitrescu was continually at the heart of the action; on this occasion the roles were reversed from the second goal when he turned provider for Hagi. If the first goal was reminiscent of Hagi's drive against Colombia, this was a throwback to the famous Carlos Alberto goal for Brazil in the Mexico 70 final. Tibor Selymes had overlapped to the left and was crying out for Dumitrescu to play him in. Instead, he waited and rolled the ball to his right where Hagi emerged and fired low past Islas to put the game out of Argentina's reach.

A late consolation from Balbo made the score more respectable but Argentina's exit was confirmed. The Romania players lifted Iordănescu aloft and threw him into the air, his tactics and system had set up a quarter-final tie again in Los Angeles with fellow surprise package Sweden. Little did Romania know that old ghosts would return to haunt them at Palo Alto's Stanford Stadium seven days later.

The adage of not changing a winning team was ignored by Iordănescu, who promptly returned Răducioiu to the starting XI at the expense of Mihali. The Swedes slowed Romania down, reducing their ability to counter-attack massively in a game where once again the crippling heat took centre stage. When Tomas Brolin gave Sweden the lead on 78 minutes it seemed that one goal would be enough. Răducioiu though had other ideas and equalised with two minutes of the 90 remaining.

Another 30 minutes in the San Francisco sun was the last thing both teams needed but in the space of 120 seconds, it looked as if the tie would fall in Romania's favour. On 100 minutes, Răducioiu scored his second of the game before Swedish enforcer Stefan Schwarz saw red for a foul on Dumitrescu shortly after. Down to ten men and with striker Martin Dahlin forced off through injury, it looked to be all over for Sweden.

Minutes later though, Prunea failed to deal with a high ball forward and allowed towering forward Kennet Andersson to head home and send the game to a penalty shoot-out. Just as they had four years earlier in Genoa, Romania faltered when it mattered most. Goalkeeper Thomas Ravelli kept out efforts from Petrescu and Belodedici, with Håkan Mild blazing over for the Swedes, who won the shoot-out 5-4.

The disappointment was too much. Many of the Romania players who had suffered the same heartbreak against Ireland sank to the ground in despair. They had come a long way in four years though and had come within five minutes of a World Cup semi-final. A quarter-final against a fellow European side was not what the likes of Lupescu wanted. 'We had hoped to play Brazil in the semi-final as we had a good record against South American teams, but we were stupid against Sweden. We had the advantage three times but couldn't manage to win. We did manage to play Brazil many years later in a veterans' game and won 4-1 but it was too late,' said Lupescu with a smile.

Also looking back the superstitious Hagi said that he feared the worst against Sweden having won at rummy the night before the game. Throughout the tournament, whenever he had lost at cards his side had gone on to win the next day.

By 1997, Romania hit the heady heights of third in the world rankings and would return to the World Cup in 1998. By the turn of the millennium, the era of Romania's greatest team was over and, despite never coming as close again, the summer of 1994 and the performance of Gheorghe Hagi would stand the test of time for decades to come.

Chapter Nine

El Diego's Last Stand

DIEGO MARADONA looked up to the stands for his wife, Claudia. Their eyes met and he gestured with a smile towards the woman who was now escorting him from the pitch as if to say, 'who's she?!' The woman was a nurse, resplendent in white with a lanyard swinging from her neck and a green cross emblazoned on her chest. Her role was to take Argentina's captain to submit a drugs test following their hard-fought match with Nigeria at the Foxboro Stadium in Massachusetts. A happy Maradona took her hand and strode off the pitch without a care in the world. Life for *El Diego* was good again, a tumultuous few years in the rear-view mirror.

It was the fourth time that the late Diego Maradona had appeared at the World Cup. It still rankled that he was overlooked for the home World Cup in 1978 with more experienced players picked ahead of the precocious 17-year-old.

The move paid off as Argentina won their first World Cup amidst one of the most politically charged tournaments ever held. By 1982, the secret was out and Maradona was expected to shine at España 82 having secured a multi-million-pound transfer to Barcelona ahead of the 1982/83 season.

However, the 1982 World Cup didn't go to plan for Maradona and he seemed to buckle under the pressure of being billed the best young footballing talent on the planet. Having finished runners-up to Belgium in the first of two group stages, *La Albiceleste* were eliminated from the latter, suffering two defeats in Barcelona, to eventual champions Italy and rivals Brazil. Four years later he would finally live up to all expectations.

The 1986 World Cup will always be remembered for Maradona's performance in the quarter-final win over England. It demonstrated the best and worst of his game as his 'hand of God' goal gave Argentina a controversial lead before he slalomed through the England team for an inconceivable second four minutes later. He realised a boyhood dream by lifting the World Cup trophy, Argentina's second, after an absorbing 3-2 win over West Germany in the final at the Estadio Azteca in Mexico City and promised that 'they' would have to tear it from his grasp at Italia 90.

The cut and thrust Argentina showed at Mexico 86 had been replaced by a more cynical unit in Italy four years later. Maradona had experienced a whirlwind four years in Italy, winning two Serie A titles with Napoli. Naples and Maradona were made for each other, a love reciprocated; to fans of *I Partenopei*, *El Diego* was God.

Argentina made their second consecutive World Cup Final where they faced a familiar foe in West Germany in a dismal match punctuated by two Argentinian dismissals, an Andreas Brehme penalty enough to ensure Argentina wouldn't repeat the feats of Mexico. The disappointed South Americans returned home as the first team to fail to score in a World Cup Final and the first defending champions to reach the final and lose.

Off the pitch, Maradona's life had begun to spiral out of control in southern Italy, his links with organised crime were now well known and his appetite for cocaine had grown exponentially. Maradona felt untouchable. He mixed with the most powerful people in the city but to those living in the slums, he could do no wrong. His house of cards came crashing down though when the government set out to smash the *Camorra* and bring an end to the organised crime syndicates that had ruled southern Italy for decades. With his protection removed, a failed drug test resulted in a 15-month ban and brought an end to Maradona and Napoli's love affair.

Whilst Maradona licked his wounds, Argentina added to their 1991 Copa América triumph by also winning the King Fahd Cup, a precursor to the Confederations Cup. Argentina were flying and under new manager Alfio 'Coco' Basile they were unbeaten in 23 matches. By this time Maradona was back playing but nowhere near his previous best. He was now in Spain with Sevilla but overweight, out of shape and approaching his 33rd birthday. The Argentine public, however, still believed in *El Diego* and, despite their successes without him, Basile recalled Maradona to the national team to face Brazil where he resumed his position as number ten and captain.

Maradona's time with Sevilla ended and he sought succour in what he knew best: cocaine. This time he was saved by his parents with whom he stayed to get clean. His career was circling the drain, he was without a club and, with the national side now boasting an array of young stars, any hopes of returning to his previous best looked slim. He gradually worked his way back to fitness and joined Newell's

Old Boys in Rosario, almost 300km (186miles) away from the distractions of Buenos Aires. Football was moving on, however, and with Newell's high-pressing style, games were passing Maradona by. As his weight fluctuated, the end looked nigh for Argentina's most famous number ten. All of that would change when *La Albiceleste* faced off against Colombia in the final South American qualifying match for USA 94, knowing they needed only a point to advance.

In the earlier stages of qualifying, Argentina had suffered a brief wobble away to Colombia followed by a draw with Paraguay which threw automatic qualification into doubt. An unthinkable defeat to Colombia at River Plate's El Monumental stadium would send Argentina into an unenviable play-off with Oceania champions Australia. Hopes for the Colombia game were high, however. Argentina would be at home and backed by a raucous partisan crowd at the home of their 1978 World Cup Final win.

Maradona was back in Buenos Aires and decided to attend the game as a fan, walking the ten blocks to the ground with his father and a friend. They joined disbelieving fans looking on as their heroes capitulated to an unfathomable 5-0 home defeat. As the goals poured in the home fans' attention turned to their former captain who was watching on in horror from an executive box. Soon the chants started: 'Maradooo, Maradoooo, Maradooooo!' The game over, a victorious Colombia celebrated qualification and left Argentina to regroup quickly as a two-legged pan-Pacific play-off with Australia awaited in two months' time.

Surprisingly Basile remained as manager, although this didn't stop a root and branch investigation into what happened on that miserable night in Buenos Aires. Argentine sports magazine *El Gráfico*'s next issue featured an all-black cover with the word *'Vergüenza'* ('disgrace') emblazoned across it. Although Basile had survived the knives were out and anything but victory over Australia would not be tolerated. The first leg was in Sydney and the under-fire manager bowed to public pressure by recalling *El Diego*. His impact was instant. Having brushed off two defenders, Maradona delivered a cross for Abel Balbo to finish. They allowed Australia back in though and Aurelio Vidmar equalised, sending the game back to Argentina and El Monumental level as *La Albiceleste* looked to vanquish the ghosts of the Colombia debacle.

Argentina did enough in the second leg, stumbling to a 1-0 win courtesy of an Alex Tobin own goal around the hour mark. Qualification was secured and a huge sigh of relief could be heard across the country. Captain on that fateful night against Colombia, Óscar Ruggeri, attested to the difference having Maradona back in the squad for the Australia games: 'After losing to Colombia we felt a lot of shame, but when Diego joined us after his sanction, we lifted ourselves up,' he said. 'We were strong as a team and Maradona covered up all that had happened, he brought us new air.'

Maradona left Newell's after playing only seven games and again found himself injured and without a club, leaving the nation's press eager to uncover his plans with the World Cup looming. He took particular umbrage with some photographers and peppered them with rubber bullets from an air rifle he kept at his country retreat, injuring four of the lensmen. Charges were pressed and Maradona was in the headlines for all of the wrong reasons again. Previously, such problems would have seen Maradona turn to cocaine. This time he had a World Cup to help focus his mind. He was severely out of shape and had run away from all responsibilities since Italia 90. USA 94 would be his last chance to lead Argentina on the world stage and one he wasn't about to give up.

Maradona travelled to Recife with the national team for a friendly with Brazil, three months before the World Cup began. He sat on Argentina's bench for only the second time in his career, overweight and miles away from where he needed to be to compete with the best. Only too aware of the situation, Maradona told Basile that he would inform him by the end of the week whether he would be available for the World Cup. Five days later the call was made. Maradona declared he would be ready and requested that he train on his own, initially to get himself up to speed before joining the rest of the squad.

Accompanied by his long-time friend and accountant Marcos Franchi, Maradona set about putting together a crack team of fitness specialists controlling everything from his diet to a workout regime. A one-week training camp was set up for a high-intensity programme that would elevate Maradona to somewhere near the same levels of fitness as his team-mates. Basile visited and enquired whether his captain would be ready for a friendly match with Morocco. He was and managed 75 minutes before being substituted, scoring a penalty in a 3-1 win. The goal was incredibly his first for Argentina since before Italia 90, having gone an incredible 1,255 minutes without finding the net for his country.

Just as normality appeared to have returned, Maradona was denied entry to Japan for a pre-World Cup tournament. In a sign of solidarity, the rest of the squad refused to travel leaving the Argentine Football Association (AFA) with little choice but to cancel the trip. Another hastily arranged tour took place involving Ecuador, Israel and Croatia, the three games split with a win, draw and defeat apiece.

Despite the chances afforded to him by Basile, Maradona was still not happy. He complained about not only the team's performance but also the itinerary of the tour, overlooking the fact that the first one to Japan was cancelled to accommodate him. Either way, the AFA appeared to listen and upon arrival ahead of the World Cup had organised for the squad to train at the privately owned Babson College 350-acre campus in New England. Perhaps with one eye on keeping Maradona out of temptation's way, the squad settled in at a Sheraton hotel on the outskirts of Boston. Maradona wasn't the only player to have courted controversy between World Cups. Caniggia had just been reinstated after serving a ban for cocaine use so both players had targets on their backs and a point to prove. Despite being winners and runners-up in the previous two finals, Argentina headed into their opening match with Greece as anything but tournament favourites.

Maradona was ready, he had lost weight and whilst he may not have had his previous physical ability, his speed of thought remained. Basile catered for him by selecting a supporting cast of willing runners in Batistuta, Caniggia and Balbo, with World Cup debutants Fernando Redondo and Diego Simeone shoring up the midfield. It seemed the perfect scenario for Maradona; Basile's instructions were clear: 'We didn't need to defend. We defended with the ball,' Maradona revealed in his autobiography, *El Diego*. 'If we keep possession of the ball and we adapt to being each other's shadow, filling in for each other, taking turns, the thing is going to work.'

Whilst Greece were anything but ideal opponents to judge against, the first game was a rousing success. In contrast to the rest of the country, the Foxboro Stadium was engulfed with downpours and both sides had to adjust to the inclement weather. Argentina settled the quicker of the two, taking the lead in only the second minute. A quick counter-attack started by Fernando Cáceres down the right side saw Maradona flick the ball back to Batistuta who bore down on the Greek goal. With a return pass to Maradona looking the more likely, goalkeeper Antonis Minou hesitated just as Athanasios Kolitsidakis lunged in. Shaken into a decision, Batistuta awkwardly poked the ball through the defender's legs and past the prone stopper into the far corner.

It was a dream start for the team in blue away shirts, who had been greeted with a ticker-tape welcome. Bits of paper clung to the damp pitch as the grey skies above threatened more rain. Argentina were cutting Greece to pieces; Batistuta was key to the chances, first getting on the end of a neat pass from Balbo only to see his shot go wide. The Roma attacker then found Maradona with a backheel who in turn released Simeone, but the man known as *Cholo* could only drive the ball wide.

The Argentine midfield dictated both the play and tempo with the Greeks some way off the pace of the game. With one minute remaining in the first half, the patient play of Redondo and Simeone released defender José Antonio Chamot who rampaged forward playing the ball into Batistuta's feet looking for a quick one-two. Instead, *Batigol* took a touch before unleashing a swerving shot with the outside of his right boot leaving Minou with no chance as the ball careered into the top corner of the goal. With 45 minutes gone, it looked as though Argentina had rediscovered their magic.

As the second half kicked off, Greece looked further and further out of their depth. Argentina toyed with them, the midfield's intricate triangles left their Greek counterparts chasing shadows, and two substitutions from manager Alketas Panagoulias did little to stem the tide. With an hour gone, Argentina scored a third. The goal was sublime, as Maradona described it in *El Diego*: 'one-touch, tac, tac, tac, like a machine gun, one-two, Redondo, me, *golazo*'. It really was that simple, a series of short passes culminated in the ball resting at Maradona's feet. He naturally shifted the ball on to his strong left side before bending a shot into the opposite corner that *Batigol* found; this time Minou could only watch. Maradona raced away in jubilation, all the pent-up anguish and frustration from the last four years was released as he roared manically down a camera lens at the side of the pitch. His eyes bulged as veins popped in his head and neck before he was embraced by his team-mates.

Caniggia and Batistuta wasted several other chances whilst Greece finally managed to muster a couple of their own. With seven minutes to go and the game won, Maradona was replaced by Ariel Ortega, touted as his heir apparent in some quarters. Batistuta rounded off the game in the last minute completing his hat-trick from the penalty spot, giving Argentina a resounding 4-0 win and three points. Despite Batistuta's goals all the talk after the game was of Maradona's return.

Nigeria were Argentina's next opponents, having also raised eyebrows in their opening-game demolition of Bulgaria. The match was touted in the *Washington Post* as being a 'changing of the guard'. After the heroics of Cameroon at Italia 90, Nigeria were eager to prove that the improvement in African football was no fluke. The early exchanges seemed to be pointing that way when Samson Siasia received the ball from striker Rashidi Yekini and lifted a shot over the advancing Luis Islas in the Argentine goal after only eight minutes, to give Nigeria the lead.

Argentina had created two chances before going behind and it wasn't long before they were level as Caniggia, who spurned several attempts against Greece, made no mistake on 22 minutes. With the ball placed for a free kick, Maradona angled to shoot but instead backheeled the ball into Batistuta's path. Peter Rufai in the Nigeria goal could only parry the stinging drive where Caniggia, anticipating a rebound, was on hand to bring Argentina level.

Maradona was conducting the orchestra in his deeper role and looked to unleash the ever-willing Caniggia down the left wing with a chipped pass before Swedish referee Bo Karlsson called play back for a free kick. Whilst the Nigerian defence organised itself, Maradona took control and rolled a pass into Caniggia, throwing the Nigerian defence off guard. Caniggia had time to look up and open his body to arch a right-footed shot around Rufai and high into the net. Argentina had turned the game around in the space of seven minutes and Nigeria looked shell-shocked.

Rufai made up for his early gaffe by denying Batistuta from adding to his first-game hat-trick, whilst the final chance of the game fell to Yekini who saw his effort snuffed out by Islas. Argentina were heading to the top of Group D with six points. Maradona was taken away for a drugs test happy that his country was performing well and, against all the odds, so was he.

As Argentina prepared for their final group match with Bulgaria, Maradona was at ease. Basile had given the squad a few hours off, away from the incessant heatwave that had engulfed most of the country. He sipped maté in the college grounds with his team-mate Sergio Goycochea and their wives. His two daughters were nearby and during games *El Diego* had taken to wearing a captain's armband with pictures of their faces on it. Perhaps Maradona should have realised that nothing in his life seemed to stay settled for long. As his friend Franchi approached, things were about to take a turn for the worse.

The drug test after the Nigeria game had come back positive. Not for cocaine, as would have been widely expected, but for a cocktail of five drugs that included ephedrine, a substance that was on FIFA's banned list. There was a second test that would be examined at a laboratory at the University of California, Los Angeles, the same used during the Olympic Games of 1984. This would eliminate any doubt there may have been with the first, but *El Diego* knew his World Cup was over.

For Maradona, first came the tears, then the anger. 'I busted my balls, I worked my arse off like never before and now this,' he documented in his autobiography. It had been reported that Maradona had lost close to 12kg in weight between joining the squad in April and the tournament opener. The Bulgaria game was the following day and would have seen Maradona make a record 22nd World Cup appearance. With the result of the second test not yet known the players set off to Dallas and by the afternoon, the squad had arrived at the Cotton Bowl to take in the surroundings ahead of their final group game. Maradona was away from the others, however, alone in his thoughts at one end of the pitch.

Shortly after 8pm, Argentine team spokesman Washington Rivera approached Maradona. After they spoke, the number ten made the sign of the cross before exiting the stadium. The news of the positive test was out, AFA president Julio Grondona appeared amongst a throng of assembled media and, pre-empting any move from FIFA, he had already removed Maradona's name from the Argentina squad list.

When Maradona faced up to the media, he pleaded his innocence, detailing all of the effort and hard work he had gone through to get to this point and swore that he hadn't taken any performance-enhancing substances. Grondona told the press that Maradona had used a nasal spray sold over the counter in Argentina which contained ephedrine. It was a claim refuted by Dr Michel d'Hooghe, a member of FIFA's executive committee, who stated that there was not one single medical product that contained the five substances that had raised the red flags on Maradona's test.

FIFA didn't state how much of each substance was in Maradona's system but ephedrine alone can increase blood pressure, heartbeat and adrenaline. It was widely included in asthma and cold cure medication but in its purest form was a go-to drug for cyclists and sprinters looking to gain an advantage. Maradona was the third player to be sent home from a World Cup after failing a drugs test; Haiti's Ernest Jean-Joseph in 1974 and Willie Johnston of Scotland four years later both fell foul of the testers.

The next day a press conference confirmed the second test was positive, just six hours before Argentina were set to take the field against Bulgaria. The previous results would stand. The tournament would go on for Argentina but not for their captain. Maradona continued to refuse accountability, accusing all and sundry of waging a plot against him, from Grondona to FIFA president João Havelange. He eventually claimed his trainer supplied him with the American version of a supplement he took in Argentina that unbeknownst to them contained ephedrine. Whatever the truth was, his Argentina career was over with another lengthy ban likely to be handed down after the World Cup.

Ruggeri was named captain for the Bulgaria game, the stalwart of three World Cups regaining the armband he had been given when Maradona returned from his previous suspension. 'I had already played in many games for Argentina,' he said. 'I felt as always that we were representing, with very few players, an entire country. I kept a cool head and tried to focus on the game.' Leonardo Rodríguez took Maradona's place in the starting XI but without him they folded, Bulgaria ran out 2-0 winners and, with Nigeria beating Greece by the same score, Argentina crept through in third place. An article in the *Los Angeles Times* wondered whether this was a blessing in disguise as Argentina avoided Italy in the last 16 and headed west to face Romania at the Rose Bowl.

Romania, led by their own Maradona of the Carpathians, Gheorghe Hagi, passed and countered *La Albiceleste* into submission in a 3-2 win regarded as one of the tournament's best games. Without Maradona, Argentina wilted. In *El Diego*, the magnitude of his absence was evident when Maradona recalled what an emotional Redondo said to him after the Bulgaria game: 'I was looking for you on the pitch and I couldn't find you. I looked for you the whole match.' Two straight defeats and for Argentina, the tournament was over.

Inexplicably Maradona remained in the USA, to commentate for TV station Channel 13, picking up a lucrative $1.3m in the process.

In his autobiography, *El Diego* spoke of how his country was robbed of their hopes and dreams as he continued to refuse to take any responsibility for his actions, an all-too-often character flaw of the man. Fans watched Argentina take Greece and Nigeria apart and anticipated them going head-to-head with the likes of Italy and Brazil later in the tournament. 'We were a team that played football very well,' said Ruggeri. 'I think if the Maradona situation hadn't happened we would have been a serious candidate to win the tournament.'

We never knew just how good that Argentina team of 1994 could have been and after the spirit-crushing exit of Maradona, we sadly never will. The enigmatic king of Argentinian football sadly passed away in November 2020 and, despite all his flaws, his contribution to the game will never be diminished.

Chapter Ten

The Best of Enemies

IN FOOTBALLING terms, Germany and the Netherlands are two sides of the same coin. Football is part of the national DNA; both are highly regarded and both have supplied some of the best players to ever grace the game. For the Germans, however, success is not only demanded but expected, whilst the Netherlands can sometimes be accused of having something of a *laissez-faire* approach. There also happens to be no love lost between the two nations which can be traced back to World War II when Germany occupied the Netherlands for five long years, having originally decimated Rotterdam to ensure a quick surrender in May 1940.

Despite this, the animosity on the football pitch did not fully begin to manifest until the 1974 World Cup, held in the then West Germany. There, the hosts defeated one of the game's most beloved Netherlands sides, led by Johan Cruyff, 2-1 in the final. Ten years later the Dutch exacted revenge to lift the Euro 88 trophy in the same stadium, their first major international honour. However, it was the semi-final in Hamburg that fans of the *Oranje* look back on with particular glee. Under the tutelage of the legendary Rinus Michels, the Dutch side led by the talented triumvirate of Ruud Gullit, Frank Rijkaard and Marco van Basten eliminated the hosts and with it laid to rest the ghosts of 1974.

Berti Vogts had stepped out of the shadow from being Franz Beckenbauer's assistant for *Die Mannschaft*, taking the reins ahead of defending their World Cup title at USA 94, now as a unified Germany. Meanwhile, the Netherlands had injected some fresh impetus to their squad with young stars like Dennis Bergkamp and Marc Overmars replacing some of the old guard. The influx of young talent was in stark contrast to their German rivals who went with the bulk of the Italia 90 squad. The fall of the Berlin Wall hadn't seen an expected influx of players from the east, with Matthias Sammer of Borussia Dortmund the obvious exception.

Despite this, the Germans' track record gave them confidence that they could defend their title. 'No defending champions had ever won two in a row,' explained assistant manager and 1974 World Cup winner Rainer Bonhof. 'We had a lot of players from Italia 90 who were keen to defend the title, but we knew it wouldn't be easy.' One thing they would have to adjust to was the sheer amount of travelling that would be required. 'There were difficult situations to handle, the USA is a huge country,' continued Bonhof. 'We had to play in Chicago, then Dallas. We're talking a four-hour flight; this was very unusual for European players.'

Ahead of USA 94, the Dutch were in need of a manager. All signs pointed towards Johan Cruyff, who had narrowly missed out on taking the job four years earlier. Back then the position was filled by Leo Beenhakker, a choice that had failed to yield any success. With Cruyff's name touted again, this time his appointment seemed a formality. According to Dennis Bergkamp's autobiography *Stillness and Speed*, one sticking point was reminiscent of an issue that occurred at the 1974 World Cup. Cruyff was once again unhappy with the brand of sportswear the Dutch would be wearing. Italian manufacturer Lotto had paid for the privilege to be the Dutch kit manufacturer but Cruyff allegedly preferred to wear his own branded clothing whilst stood on the sidelines.

Technology or lack thereof also played its part. In these pre-internet times, the Royal Dutch Football Association (KNVB) preferred to conduct its negotiations with Cruyff via fax machine. Cruyff, however, claimed he was unable to use one and left the negotiations to third parties. When issues arose over money, both parties had had enough. Talks broke down and the dream of Cruyff leading the *Oranje* at a World Cup was over. The KNVB moved on and gave the job to Dick Advocaat, who had spent some of his playing career in the USA. According to Dutch winger Bryan Roy, this was a huge missed opportunity. 'It wasn't to be, in 1990 or 94. Cruyff had always had a love/hate relationship with the KNVB but things had to go his way, he had to be right,' Roy said. Would the appointment of Cruyff have made the difference? 'Always,' Roy concluded. 'He was a genius.'

Meanwhile, Vogts replaced Beckenbauer immediately after Italia 90 hoping to join *Der Kaiser* in winning a World Cup as both a player and manager. Whilst he had kept Germany at the top of the world's rankings, losing the final of Euro 92 to late additions Denmark had seen pressure begin to build on the shoemaker's son who was nicknamed 'the Terrier' during his playing career with Borussia Mönchengladbach.

A victory at Euro 92 would have cemented Vogts's place amongst his numerous predecessors who had all won a World Cup or European Championship whilst in charge of *Die Mannschaft*. Vogts had received the benefit of the doubt following the Denmark defeat in 1992 and, having been drawn in a favourable group with Bolivia, Spain and South Korea, a place in the knockout stages looked a formality.

Germany would be kicking off the tournament and Vogts was eager to make an early statement. A month before proceedings got underway, Vogts set up a gruelling training camp for his squad in Malente, northern Germany. The squad were put through their paces, including energy-sapping triple training sessions. Some members of the squad reacted negatively, with Vogts pulling several into his office to chastise them over their conduct. The stakes could not have been any higher: Germany could become the first nation to retain a World Cup and Vogts didn't want to carry any passengers.

Despite his desire to make USA 94, van Basten simply wasn't fit enough to make the Netherlands squad. The ankle injuries that would eventually curtail his career were beginning to take their toll. Gullit, who was frozen out at Milan, had enjoyed a renaissance on loan at Sampdoria but surprisingly declared his unavailability for the World Cup at a press conference. The hordes of Dutch fans reeled in shock as speculation mounted that the Euro 88 captain had fallen out with Advocaat about tactics, whilst the gossip columns suggested his no-show was more to do with the demands of his girlfriend. Whatever the truth may have been, one thing was for certain: the Dutch would be without two of their key men from the previous six years.

The remaining players shrugged off their absence, buoyed by the addition of the de Boer twins, Frank and Ronald. However, despite the attacking threat of Bergkamp and Overmars, they shifted the dynamic of the national team. A 3-0 win over Canada in a pre-tournament friendly left swathes of the Dutch press dismissive of Advocaat's side with pronouncements of 'boring' football shocking many of the players. The tag hurt that much that the rift between players and press continued into the tournament with many of the Dutch squad making themselves unavailable for interviews.

The 1994 World Cup finally got underway at Chicago's Soldier Field with Germany clear favourites against Bolivia, who were making their first World Cup appearance in 44 years.

German defender and scorer of the winning goal at Italia 90, Andreas Brehme, was confident his side wouldn't wilt under both the expectations and the heat. 'When you are playing for the German national team there is always a lot of pressure on the players since people expect you to at least reach the final,' he explained. 'When you are a defender, the pressure is even higher. Since all of us were playing at top clubs we were used to performing under this pressure and could handle it. We couldn't complain about the kick-off times or heat either, it was the same for all of the teams and we just had to deal with it.'

Something of an unknown quantity outside of South America, Bolivia were cheered by the return of their star player, Marco Etcheverry, who had managed to overcome an injury to make the bench. If *La Verde* were to pull off a shock akin to Cameroon beating Argentina in the opening game of Italia 90, they would need their tousle-haired talisman at his best.

'We had a lot of information on them. The head coach [Xabier Azkargorta] was also a friend of mine,' remembered Bonhof. 'We had sent a scout to watch them at the Copa América in 1993 whilst myself and Berti had also watched them in person. We perhaps didn't have as much information as we would today, but we had scouts all around the world.'

The Netherlands also opened their World Cup campaign against another of the tournament minnows, debutants

Saudi Arabia. With the introduction of three points for a win, FIFA had hoped there would be more of a gung-ho approach to games. However, in some quarters it had the opposite effect as teams adopted a more cautious approach since an opening defeat left teams on the precipice of going home. The caution may have subtracted from the spectacle but, in this case, both Germany and the Netherlands came through with narrow wins.

Germany had won the tournament's opening game 1-0, with Jürgen Klinsmann grabbing the only goal just after the hour mark. Captain Lothar Matthäus, who had been deployed in a sweeper role, hooked forward a high ball as the Bolivian defence rushed out, looking to play offside. The ball fell on to the chest of midfielder Thomas Häßler who inadvertently played it into Klinsmann's path. With onrushing Bolivian goalkeeper Carlo Trucco caught out of position, the blond striker stroked the ball into an empty net.

The sense of relief in taking the lead was clear; the 32°C heat had seen the game being played at a pedestrian pace. Any hopes Bolivia may have carried when Etcheverry came on in the second half were extinguished when he saw red for lashing out a mere three minutes after being introduced. A dismissal for violent conduct meant an automatic three-match ban and Bolivia's main star saw his World Cup was over before it had truly begun. Over in Group F, the Netherlands fell behind early to a shock goal from Saudi Arabia's Fuad Amin before order was restored in the second half. Goals from Wim Jonk and substitute Gaston Taument at the RFK Stadium in Washington DC secured the three points. It was a case of 'job done' but still a far from cogent start for two of European football's heavyweights.

More familiar opponents lay in wait as Germany stayed in Chicago to play Spain whilst the Netherlands moved to Orlando where they faced neighbours Belgium. If the performances in the first games were put down to nerves, then those in the second gave a cause for concern. Firstly, Germany played out a fortuitous 1-1 draw with a Spanish side still more than a decade away from being the force that won a World Cup and two European Championships. 'It was a very intensive game for us,' explained Brehme. 'The draw was fine for us since we were confident of reaching the last eight with a victory in our final group game.' The Netherlands, meanwhile, suffered the ignominy of losing 1-0 to the Belgians, defender Philippe Albert scoring the only goal. Belgium had goalkeeper Michel Preud'homme to thank for the three points as his performance here went a long way to cementing his place in the World Cup's team of the tournament.

The experienced names Vogts had opted for when naming his squad were proving to be their Achilles heel. Germany's ageing defence had withered in the heat late in the Spain game and with an energetic South Korea side standing in their way of making the knockout stages they were finding the challenge of defending their title a lot harder than they initially envisaged.

All these concerns were blown away in the first half of their final group game when *Die Mannschaft* raced into a three-goal lead, powered once again by the goals of Klinsmann, who bagged a brace. The inexperienced Koreans, who had yet to win a World Cup game, could have folded but instead came roaring back, goals from Seon-Hong Hwang and Myung-Bo Hong providing hope.

The Germans were hanging on. 'Korea were dominating us,' said an exasperated Bonhof. The beleaguered Stefan Effenberg had been hauled off with 15 minutes to go. 'It was difficult for him, he was playing out of position but should have handled the situation better,' Bonhof added. The whistles and catcalls from the travelling German fans were too much for the Fiorentina man who gestured in their direction, an act which would see him exit the tournament in shame afterwards. 'We gave him an option to apologise to the fans which he refused, so we sent him home,' Bonhof concluded unapologetically.

German goalkeeper Bodo Illgner's selection had been called into question after his role in Spain's goal six days earlier, but he ensured Germany hung on to seal their place in the knockouts. Another far from convincing performance from the holders was not helped by the early exit of Matthäus who was substituted with a badly cut foot.

The surprising performances of Saudi Arabia had kept Group F wide open with three teams still able to qualify heading into the last group game. The Dutch, who would once again play in Orlando, this time against Morocco, could still win the group or if results went against them head home. 'As a group, we were improving but the heat was killing us,' said Roy who scored in the Morocco game. 'It was constant, during training, games, everything and in Orlando, it was even worse.'

The Africans were missing their star man, Nourredine Naybet, who was suspended after picking up a second yellow card against Saudi Arabia. His absence seemed apparent when Bergkamp opened the scoring two minutes before half-time only for Hassan Nader to draw Morocco level the other side of the break. Roy's goal secured the three points and his country's passage into the next round where a tie with the Republic of Ireland awaited. 'It was very special to score a goal in a World Cup,' said Roy, 'even more so to make it 2-1 in a game we needed to win.' As the group stages came to an end both Germany and the Netherlands had advanced as expected but both looked fallible, one slip now and their tournament would be over.

Things hadn't gone as expected thus far, but the common consensus was that the performances of both sides would improve as the tournament went on. This certainly seemed the case with the Netherlands as they swept Jack Charlton's Ireland aside with ease in Orlando, Bergkamp again amongst the goals as they booked themselves a place in the quarter-finals against Brazil in Dallas.

Germany headed back to Chicago where they faced Belgium on a day where the World Cup woke to the news of Andrés Escobar's callous murder back in Colombia. Both teams immaculately observed a minute's silence in the Colombian's honour before kick-off. A European opponent was certainly welcome, having played Bolivia and South Korea in two of their last three games. Matthäus was given 45 minutes after warily returning to the side after injury.

Whilst Klinsmann got on the scoresheet once more it was the oldest member of the squad, Rudi Völler, who would put the Germans through. The striker's brace secured a 3-2 win that sent Belgium home aggrieved at Swiss referee Kurt Röthlisberger for first failing to award them a second-half penalty and not giving German defender Thomas Helmer a second yellow card in the process.

Both sides were now two games away from the final and, being on opposite sides of the draw, that was the only place they could meet. The Netherlands would have to defeat the tournament favourites, Brazil, a difficult task made all the harder when the team plane was left on the tarmac for hours after a member of the Dutch press joked about having a bomb in his luggage. 'The delay didn't affect the team that much, but it did spook Dennis,' said Roy. Bergkamp's fear of flying was well documented and this was the last thing he needed heading into the biggest game of his career so far.

Germany left their second home of Chicago to head to New Jersey's Giants Stadium to face tournament surprise package Bulgaria. One man missing was the injured Sammer who had proved to be a vital cog in the German machine, with Matthäus now back to full fitness and accustomed to his deeper role. 'Sammer was still a young player having come into the set up quickly after the wall came down,' explained Bonhof. 'He organised things in the midfield, but we had so many good players we should have been able to win this match.'

They were clear favourites and, as expected, all the statistics pointed to a Germany win. They had reached five of the previous seven World Cup finals, including the previous three. The Germans had not tasted defeat at a World Cup since the final of Mexico 86 and Bulgaria were coming off a gruelling 120-minute encounter against *El Tri* in which they had needed a penalty shoot-out to advance.

For the Netherlands, if they could circumvent Brazil at the Cotton Bowl an appetising semi-final match-up awaited against either Sweden or Romania. The Dutch, bedecked in their white away shirts, eased the ball around looking to pick holes in the Brazilian lines. The style was ingrained, Advocaat choosing only two players who had not been schooled in the Ajax system, and one of them was goalkeeper Ed de Goey.

Whilst Brazilian sides of yore had more flair than this one, they also had a soft underbelly, something which coach Carlos Alberto Parreira looked to erase. They coped with the Dutch, keeping them at arm's length whilst looking to release the strike duo of Romário and Bebeto. In 30 second-half minutes, the game exploded in a barrage of goals, the

Diabolical Duo giving Brazil a seemingly unassailable 2-0 lead with a little under half an hour to play.

For the second goal, the Dutch defence waited for an offside flag that never came and FIFA's new interpretation of the rule left many scratching their heads in confusion. Referee Rodrigo Badilla adjudged Romário to have not interfered with play so the game continued and the Dutch were two goals down. The Netherlands struck back, however, with goals from Bergkamp and Aron Winter, who levelled proceedings on 76 minutes.

In New Jersey, Germany took the lead from the penalty spot shortly after the half-time break. Matthäus stroked home from the spot in his record-equalling 21st World Cup match after Bulgaria's Yordan Letchkov was adjudged to have fouled Klinsmann in the box. There would be no appearance record for Matthäus, however, as the profligate Germans failed to add to their lead. In the blink of an eye the game was turned on its head as Bulgaria struck twice in three minutes to secure the shock of the tournament. Striker Hristo Stoichkov and the aforementioned Letchkov grabbed the goals to stun the thousands of Germans in attendance.

With the scores level at the Cotton Bowl, extra time beckoned until Brazilian defender Branco, only playing due to first-choice left-back Leonardo's suspension, drilled a free kick into the corner of de Goey's goal. It was Branco's first game in a month and the goal allowed him the last laugh on those who expected Overmars to run him ragged all game. The result ensured no repeat of the 1974 World Cup Final and similar to Euro 88, a final containing two of football's fiercest rivals had been snatched away. Losing a big game was still a rarefied experience for many of the German squad but for the Dutch, it was something they had become all too accustomed to over the years. Advocaat raised eyebrows after the game by admitting he was pleased to finish within the top eight teams at the tournament.

'We had a very good squad, I believe if we had got past Brazil we would have won the tournament,' said Roy. 'The fans were terrific, there was an unbelievable amount of them there and they were always positive. Football-wise, we were one of the best around, Ajax won the European Cup the next year. We had made the last four of Euro 92 and then the quarter-finals at the World Cup, we were just not good enough at that precise moment.'

For Germany, after the disappointment of Euro 92, the knives were out for Vogts and his coaching staff. 'For me, the referee was not on the level needed for such an important match,' ventured Bonhof. 'Everyone expected us to make the final, so we were blamed for everything. We went our separate ways when we came home before giving interviews with the press that had to be done. As expected, it was not a warm reception.'

Vogts and his assistant rode the storm and surprisingly kept their jobs. 'We renovated the squad, had knowledge of how to handle players at a tournament and organised evenings to help generate team spirit,' Bonhof explained. For Brehme, though, the answer was clear. 'In 1990, everything was perfect which you need to become world champion,' he explained. 'Four years later we were only at 90 per cent and that is not enough.'

One matter that had caused some consternation amongst the squad in the USA was Vogts not allowing the players to spend time with their wives and girlfriends. 'We knew we had to do more for the team spirit and heading into Euro 96 we allowed the players a day off after matches to be with their wives,' added Bonhof. An approach that worked as Germany helped themselves to their third European Championship in England two years on from USA 94.

Chapter Eleven

Life Does Not End Here

IT WAS 3.30am on 2 July 1994 when the phone rang. It shattered the early-morning silence and startled María Ester Escobar from her slumber. She stared at the phone knowing that when she answered her life would change forever. On the other end of the line was Gabriel *'Barrabás'* Gómez, a friend and team-mate of her brother Andrés. His voice cracked as he broke the news: 'Maria, something terrible has happened. It's Andrés, he has been killed.'

In a nightclub car park in downtown Medellín, a crowd had gathered. Sirens could be heard in the distance as police officers desperately tried to move people away from a stationary car, the blood-soaked driver's seat visible through the shattered glass. The car belonged to son of the city Andrés Escobar, footballer for Atlético Nacional and proud owner of 51 Colombia caps.

Escobar had been shot six times in the back after becoming embroiled in an argument as he left the nightclub and was pronounced dead in a nearby hospital. It appeared that the source of the fatal argument stemmed from events that happened ten days earlier and over 3,000 miles away during his 50th appearance for Colombia. In their second game, Colombia faced hosts, the USA. Although heavy favourites, everything changed after 35 minutes.

USA midfielder John Harkes broke from midfield with Colombian defenders ahead of him. As Harkes hit a low cross towards the penalty area Escobar knew there was an attacker, Earnie Stewart, behind him. Sensing Stewart had got ahead of his marker, Escobar had no choice but to make a play at the ball. At full stretch, his right boot connected near the penalty spot. Óscar Córdoba had followed the ball's trajectory and was in no man's land. Escobar could only lay prone on the ground and watch as the ball rolled into the unguarded net.

The composed defender who was born in the Calasanz neighbourhood of Medellín was known to fans as *El Caballero del Fútbol* ('the gentleman of football'). A young Escobar took school seriously, but it wasn't long before a burgeoning talent for football took over his life. He came to a fork in the road where he had to choose between furthering his education or his football career, finally deciding on the latter.

Scouts and coaches had already spotted his potential, admiring his calm demeanour on the pitch combined with excellent leadership skills. Atlético Nacional head coach Francisco Maturana had seen enough and signed the 19-year-old defender to play for Medellín's premier club. Maturana was destined to become a pivotal figure in Colombian football over the next decade as Bogotá-based British journalist Carl Worswick explained: 'Maturana was a dentist and was still practising even when he became a manager. That made him a bit more outward looking than other Colombian coaches. He was a bit braver in trying new ideas, in absorbing things he had seen in other fields and incorporating them into football.'

Maturana took over the national team in 1987, having ruled the roost with Atlético Nacional leading them to victory in the Copa Libertadores during his time there. Football was becoming a way of life in Medellín, but during the 1990s the capital of Colombia's Antioquia province known as the 'City of Eternal Spring' was the most dangerous place on earth. During 1994 alone there were 266 murders per 100,000 people in the country, a terrifying statistic that was mirrored across the country. Violence and murder had become an everyday part of life in Colombia, the drug cartels of Cali and Medellín had seen to that. The latter's kingpin, Pablo Escobar, had declared war on the government but since his death, in a shoot-out on the rooftops of Medellín the previous December, the lawlessness on the streets had spiralled out of control.

Cocaine had become big business in Colombia, with the Medellín cartel making an estimated $50m a day exporting the drug around the globe. Drug lord Pablo Escobar was a hero to the people of Medellín, providing homes and a better quality of life for the residents of his home city. He built numerous football pitches across the area too, many of which played host to young boys who would go on to star for their country. On top of this, Escobar satisfied his love of football by ploughing his ill-gotten gains into Atlético Nacional; a quick and easy way to legalise the drug money that was flooding in and giving birth to the era of 'Narco-Soccer'.

'One of the consequences of the increasing involvement of the drug money in the domestic game was it attracted big stars to play in the Colombian league,' explained Worswick. 'High wages which were usually paid in dollars and declared in pesos ensured that Colombia's best players also stayed. Interest grew, rivalries developed, stadiums filled up and football became much more important within Colombian society.'

It wasn't uncommon for Atlético Nacional players to spend time in Pablo Escobar's presence, an invite to his lavish soirées something not wise to turn down. National team goalkeeper René Higuita was unwisely caught on film visiting the cartel leader whilst he was imprisoned. As Escobar's wealth and notoriety grew so did the violence. Explosions rocked the city as the Medellín cartel upped the stakes by planting bombs as a warning for the authorities to divert their gaze elsewhere. The government had seen enough though and the battle to end the murderous grip of the drug cartels began.

The increased investment in football had paid dividends, however, with the national team reaching the Copa América semi-finals three times between 1987 and 1991. They also qualified for their second World Cup in 1990 as an array of star players began to emerge. Domestically, Atlético Nacional became the first Colombian side to win the Copa Libertadores in 1989, beating Paraguay's Club Olimpia on penalties with Andrés Escobar scoring the first attempt of the shoot-out.

The 1990 World Cup came to a disappointing early end as the unpredictable Higuita gifted a goal to Cameroon's Roger Milla to seal their fate. The progress was evident, however, and *Los Cafeteros* headed into the qualifiers for USA 94 confident they could unseat Brazil and Argentina as the main players in South American football. The notoriously difficult CONMEBOL qualifiers were the perfect place for Colombia to show 'the big two' just how much they had improved.

Maturana was now the national manager and boasted a side made up of some of the best to ever pull on the yellow shirt. In June 1993, Higuita was arrested having acted as a go-between for a kidnapping, his friendship with Pablo Escobar putting something of a target on his back with the police. A ten-year prison sentence was mooted but Higuita subsequently spent a mere seven months behind bars but missed vital qualifiers and ultimately a place at the World Cup.

Colombia had already defeated Argentina in the first round of qualifying games when they secured a 2-1 win in the Caribbean port city of Barranquilla. The return game would decide who would be heading to the 1994 World Cup and who would be forced to endure a gruelling two-legged play-off against the winner of Oceania Football Confederation (OFC) qualifying, Australia.

Maturana's side was unbeaten so far in qualifying and had reached 19th spot in the FIFA world rankings. The win in Barranquilla had also ended Argentina's own 33-match unbeaten run that stretched back to the 1990 World Cup Final. A win or draw would be enough to secure *Los Cafeteros'* place at USA 94, but the omens weren't on their side as Argentina were yet to lose a World Cup qualifier on home soil.

Maturana had masterminded an attacking brand of football that had allowed Colombia to cruise their way through qualifying. Higuita's replacement, 23-year-old America de Cali goalkeeper Óscar Córdoba, played behind a defence made up entirely of players who all starred in the Colombian top flight. Flamboyant captain Carlos Valderrama ran the show in midfield whilst the attacking threat was provided by Faustino Asprilla, Adolfo '*El Tren*' Valencia and Freddy Rincón. Despite the steady flow of cash running throughout Colombian football this trio had all gone to play abroad with Parma in Italy, Germany's Bayern Munich and Palmeiras of Brazil respectively.

Before the deciding game, the South American press were eager for Diego Maradona's take. The Argentine legend was absent from the squad but, ever the showman, shared his views. 'Argentina are up here,' he said gesturing a high line in the air. 'Colombia are down there,' he concluded, pointing to a spot several feet lower. Maradona's view was a common one throughout South American football. 'Up until the 1980s, Colombian football hadn't really developed its own unique identity,' said Worswick, whose work appears in *World Soccer* and *The Guardian* amongst others.

After a fitful first half-hour, the game sparked into life when Colombia won a throw-in deep in opposition territory. Argentina failed to clear their lines and a weak defensive header landed at the feet of Valderrama. The frizzy-haired Atlético Junior man slid the ball through to an onrushing Rincón who, with one touch, rounded Sergio Goycochea and finished with ease. The half-time whistle blew and Colombia were 45 minutes away from qualifying for their third World Cup, although no one could have foreseen just how the second half would play out.

Five minutes after the restart Rincón turned provider when he lofted an angled ball to striker Asprilla. The Parma man beat his marker and fired a low shot under the advancing Goycochea. It was 2-0 and the fans in El Monumental had been stunned into silence. Still, *Los Cafeteros* attacked, looking to finish their opponents off. Argentina themselves did manage to create some chances as they went for broke to get back into the game, but it was Colombia and Rincón who got the all-important third goal. The scoring didn't stop there though; Asprilla scored his second and Colombia's fourth two minutes later as the crowd looked on helplessly. The Colombian bench emptied as celebrations erupted at what was unfolding. There was even time for a fifth goal, this time Valencia raced on to a Valderrama through ball and cheekily dinked an effort over the hapless Goycochea.

Following the rout, celebrations continued long into the night back in Colombia as a third South American superpower appeared to be emerging with even Pelé providing his seal of approval ahead of the World Cup. 'For me, Colombia is the best team. It doesn't mean they are going to win it, but they will be one of the four semi-finalists,' the Brazilian legend said assuredly. The shock result rightfully sealed its place in the annals of Colombian football history; *El Cinco-Cero* is celebrated in Colombia on the anniversary of that cold Sunday evening in Buenos Aires.

The aftereffects of the result would resonate for years to come. 'Nobody knew how to deal with it and within the tumultuous context of what was going on in Colombian society at that time, everything then spun out of control,' said Worswick. 'I suppose it was like a teenage kid getting to number one with his first single and seeing his life change overnight, without anyone to put the brakes on or offer level-headed guidance.'

Thanks to his appearance, the press throng were like moths to Valderrama's flame. The softly spoken man known as *El Pibe* had first come to the world's attention at Italia 90. Valderrama had enjoyed spells in French and Spanish football and he knew that his previous World Cup experience would be invaluable if Colombia were to live up to the increased expectations. For the players, this was an opportunity to show the world that there was more to Colombia than drugs and violence.

A lot can happen in six months, however, and suddenly things started to go wrong for Colombia. First came the end of their 28-game unbeaten streak, shattered during a friendly defeat to Bolivia. Then their World Cup kits were stolen. Finally, the infant son of defender Luis 'Chonto' Herrera was kidnapped in Medellín before being safely returned. 'After the Argentina result, players had cashed in as their egos ballooned, business and political interests meddled with the side and nobody was able to repress the monster that the result had given birth to,' said Worswick.

The Colombian Football Federation didn't help, organising over 30 warm-up games after the 5-0 win. Special packages were sold which allowed the fans to stay at the same hotel as the players. Tours were arranged for the Middle East and the US, with Asprilla using some of his Italian contacts to also get some club sides over to Colombia. 'Nobody wanted to burst the bubble, so games were deliberately arranged against poor sides, or even B teams,' Worswick explained. 'If anybody needs a blueprint on how not to prepare for a World Cup then Colombia's preparation for USA 94 is a pretty good guide, for a few months Colombia became the football world's Harlem Globetrotters.'

With things threatening to spiral out of control, the cartel's presence was felt at every turn. Some players later admitted they had been to meet the Cali cartel bosses to discuss potential bonuses for their World Cup performances. The emphatic qualifying victory over Argentina had blown everything out of proportion which, when coupled with Pelé's prediction, had seen the hype machine go into overdrive as Colombia arrived at the Fullerton Marriott hotel in Orange County, California.

Rumour had it the players had grown so confident in their abilities that allegedly two mainstays of their World Cup preparation were alcohol and women. Maturana, however, was realistic and played down his country's chances at any opportunity he got. 'For me, the important thing is to compete, to leave a mark, a footprint,' he told a reporter when arriving in the States.

Whilst showing promise at the last World Cup, those players were now four years older. Valderrama was 32 and returning from a nagging injury whilst Asprilla and Valencia had only recently completed punishing seasons in Europe. Rincón's form had dipped in Brazil and he arrived at the World Cup desperate to rediscover his best. There were talks of cliques within the squad too; the Atlético Nacional players stuck together, the serious Valderrama and gregarious Asprilla were like chalk and cheese.

Their opening game of the World Cup was against Romania at the Rose Bowl in Pasadena, the stadium where many assumed Colombia would receive their World Cup crown in 28 days' time. Maturana's plan of controlling possession played straight into Romania's hands as Anghel Iordănescu's men waited patiently before pouncing on loose balls and launching a series of counter-attacks. Colombia had seen the better of the early exchanges but found Romania goalkeeper Bogdan Stelea in imperious form. After the initial wave of Colombia attacks subsided and Valderrama was nullified, the Romanians found their usual creative outlet: the mercurial genius of Gheorghe Hagi.

On 16 minutes, Hagi, the Romania captain, released striker Florin Răducioiu following a neat side-step dummy. The AC Milan striker still with plenty to do cut inside on to his right foot and lashed a shot past Córdoba into the goal to make it 1-0. Stelea came to Romania's rescue once more, clawing the ball wide from a Valencia effort, before Hagi had Córdoba scrambling with an attempted lob that he managed to tip wide.

If Higuita's replacement was helpless for the first goal he certainly had to take some responsibility for the second. Hagi received the ball out wide and with one swing of his wand-like left foot sent a looping effort high over the advanced Córdoba and just inside the far post. It was 2-0 with 34 minutes on the clock and it already looked a long way back for Maturana's men.

With time running out in the first half, Hagi was on the receiving end of a stern challenge from Gómez, needing one of the new electronic carts to take him off the field for treatment. It was while Hagi was absent that Colombia got a foothold back in the game. An inswinging corner from Wilson Pérez was met by the head of Valencia and Stelea was only able to palm the ball into the roof of the net.

Being behind to Romania was Colombia's worst nightmare; the eastern Europeans were highly organised, compact and ready to counter-attack. Facing Stelea in the form of his life, Colombia could not find a way through. With two minutes remaining Hagi and Răducioiu combined once more. Córdoba suffered a Higuita-esque rush of blood and advanced from his goal as Răducioiu nicked the ball past him and stroked it into the empty net.

The game was over and the large Colombian support left the Rose Bowl in disbelief. Despite being undone by a Romanian side with a perfectly executed game plan, Maturana felt the result could have been different if only they had converted one of their many early chances.

Back in Colombia, however, the Romania defeat had set alarm bells ringing. 'Nobody expected it and so it was a huge shock. Colombia had played pretty well and could consider themselves unlucky to have lost,' remembered Worswick. Nobody knew how to respond though. Maturana rang his friend, Italy coach Arrigo Sacchi, that night seeking advice.

Italy too had lost their opening game to less illustrious opponents. 'Sacchi told him not to worry, that they'd been unlucky and would undoubtedly bounce back, because that's what great teams do,' said Worswick. 'They had no experience of this type of situation though and there was no mental strength to overcome it. Preparation were disastrous and continued to be so, really the damage had already been done.'

During the build-up to their now vital second game against the USA, the Colombian media spoke of a 'dark hand' at play. Firstly, news came through that Herrera's brother had been killed in a car accident, whilst Medellín spent most evenings ablaze. The death of Pablo Escobar in December 1993 had left something of a power vacuum in the city. Investigations were constantly frustrated, and authorities appeared powerless to do anything about it. The cartels evolved and were always one step ahead of the authorities.

It was the day of the USA game and the Colombia squad were readying themselves in the team hotel when the *'terrorismo telefónico'* occurred. Colombian newspaper *La Prensa* later identified a 'shadowy death squad' who sent faxes and made phone calls to the team hotel, namely to Maturana and defender Barrabás Gómez, brother of assistant coach Hernán Darío, known throughout the game as *Bolillo*.

'There will be bombs in your house and Gómez's house if you put him on the field,' the caller stated. Further threats were made that involved the rest of the squad. With two hours to go before kick-off, Maturana revealed the news to the squad. The safety of his players was paramount and he eventually ceded to the demands leaving Gómez out of the side. Maturana then broke down and stated he would be stepping down as manager at the end of the tournament.

The players had become used to the violence in their country but now it was too close to home. Maturana called *Bolillo* to his room to discuss whether they could not play the game. Further meetings took place with the players and fearing other reprisals if they didn't the players took to the pitch desperately trying to focus on the job in hand. Shockingly, Asprilla later stated he feared the players could be sitting ducks for an assassin's bullet as they lined up for the national anthems before kick-off. Hernán Gaviria, who would tragically die on the pitch in 2002 after being struck by lightning, took Gómez's place. Any concerns about Colombia's mental state looked unfounded as they raced out of the traps, bombarding the USA goal from the first whistle. With minds racing, *Los Cafeteros'* attacks were frantic but, as with the Romania game, the opposition goal seemed impenetrable.

During the early exchanges, Colombia's best chance came when USA midfielder Mike Sorber chested the ball against his own post with Marcelo Balboa luckily on hand to clear off the line. One bounce the other way would have given Colombia a deserved lead and with it released some of the pressure on the players. It wasn't to be though, and as time passed, the USA grew more and more into the game eventually taking the lead thanks to Escobar's contretemps.

Whilst the Rose Bowl erupted in celebration, the significance of what had happened hit the Colombians. Instead of galvanising them, everything unravelled with Stewart adding another seven minutes into the second half. Maturana told journalists after the game he would have changed all 11 players at the break if he could have. The best Colombia could muster was a 90th-minute consolation goal from Valencia. The USA had defied all odds and beaten the South Americans and barring a miracle one of the pre-tournament favourites would exit at the group stage.

Back home the fury of fans was evident as they jammed local radio phone-ins with their conspiracy theories. These ranged from the players being doped to throwing the game as part of a gambling ring. Police set up armed guards around the homes of Maturana and Gómez as the news broke to Colombians that their national team had been sabotaged by a home-grown terror group.

Word also spread of Maturana's impending exit from the national team. He told the press he had come to his decision before arriving in the USA but the timing of the announcement only added to the air of despondency. The players had gone into their shells and unsurprisingly no one was willing to speak to the press about the threats or what was happening behind the scenes.

In football terms, the facts were clear. Colombia were bottom of Group A, needing to beat Switzerland in the final game and hoping that the USA could pull off another win, this time over Romania. Sensing this was the final throw of the dice, Colombia played with more freedom creating numerous chances and produced some of the tournament's most exciting football so far. However, news filtered through that Romania had taken an early lead against the USA. Colombia's chances were dwindling.

Hope arrived just before half-time when Gaviria found the net, heading past Marco Pascolo from a Valderrama free kick. The Swiss goalkeeper, who had stood firm to a first-half barrage from Colombia, half-heartedly appealed for offside but to no avail. Young substitute Harold Lozano added another in second-half injury time but with no further goals in the other game, it was all in vain. Colombia had finished bottom of Group A and were the first team to be eliminated from the tournament.

Sensing the atmosphere back home, Maturana advised his squad to remain in the USA, at least until the situation calmed down. Escobar, having previously appeared in numerous television commercials, had been offered a pundit's role by TV network Caracol for the remainder of the tournament. He declined, saying he wanted to return to Colombia. He felt he had done nothing wrong. In football sometimes things didn't go your way, he thought. His parents had arrived in the USA and had planned to stay and take a tour of the country, but he was adamant he wanted to go home.

The previous two weeks had been a nightmare; Escobar craved normality as soon as possible. Escobar felt safe in Medellín, it was his home city and his performances with Atlético Nacional had always won him admirers. He had received two offers before the World Cup began, one from Mexico and the other from Italian giants AC Milan. Despite the love for his city, he had decided to move to Italy and would marry his fiancée Pamela Cascardo later that year. He had a regular column in national newspaper *El Tiempo* in which he vowed to continue writing despite the World Cup disappointment.

A week after Colombia's exit, Escobar planned to meet with friends in downtown Medellín. Cascardo was uneasy, wanting her fiancé to stay home and keep a low profile until the dust had settled. Her concerns were shared by Escobar's team-mate Herrera, who turned down the offer of meeting with him. Escobar wanted to show his face in the city, he was adamant he would not hide away.

The first signs of trouble in El Indio nightclub came when a group of revellers began insulting Escobar, sarcastically cheering and congratulating him on the own goal. Aiming to defuse the situation, Escobar left the nightclub and got into his car as the group reappeared, sending further insults his way.

In a decision that cost his life, Escobar drove across the car park to reason with the men. A .38-calibre gun appeared and six bullets were fired into Escobar. Eyewitnesses described hearing the assailant shout '*gol*' with each pull of the trigger. The gang fled; an ambulance raced Escobar to a nearby hospital where he was pronounced dead 30 minutes later.

The following morning the news broke stateside with players, journalists and officials all gathered in disbelief. Until this point the World Cup had been a huge celebration, stadiums had been full and the USA finally seemed to be welcoming football into its everyday consciousness. Now, though, it appeared that an incident during one of the games had contributed to a player being murdered.

Initial rumours suggested Escobar's murder was a reaction to huge gambling losses the drug cartels had suffered following the USA defeat. A licence plate of the assailants was traced to Pedro and Juan Gallón, two drug traffickers who had defected from the Medellín cartel. One of their bodyguards took the rap and was sentenced to 43 years in prison, only to be released after serving 11. The Gallón brothers were cleared of any part in the murder.

Over 100,000 people filed past Escobar's body as he lay in state at a Medellín basketball arena with President César Gaviria asking for Colombians to be more tolerant of each other. Thousands of mourners lined the streets sporting the green and white of Atlético Nacional whilst chanting 'Justice, justice.' Flowers were thrown at the hearse as Escobar was taken to his final resting place, with an estimated 15,000 people in attendance to see his coffin lowered into the ground.

The murder of Andrés Escobar sent shockwaves not only through football but also around the world. 'What Pablo Escobar's death did was to unleash a mad scramble for control of his drug empire, especially in Medellín. The months that ensued saw drug *capos* battle for power and thus unbridle the chaos and violence that Andrés Escobar stepped back into when he returned from the USA,' said Worswick. On the surface, the cold-blooded murder of the defender seemed to begin a time of healing in Medellín, a city now known as having one of South America's fastest-growing economies.

In 2013, it was hailed as 'the most innovative city in the world', far removed from its murderous past. Worswick though has other thoughts: 'The violence still continues, Colombia still produces most of the world's cocaine and huge parts of Medellín are still controlled by drug cartels despite what the tourist campaigns say,' he said. 'You cut off one head and several more immediately appear. What the murder of Escobar did do though was hammer home how absurd the situation had become. If even the famous "Gentleman of Football", a quiet, middle-classed lad who almost always kept his head down could end up in the wrong place at the wrong time, then it could happen to any Colombian.'

The death threats were roundly blamed for contributing to Colombia's World Cup exit but, for others, the beginning of the end could be traced back to the famous qualifying victory over Argentina. In his autobiography *El Diego*, Diego Maradona said that Colombia had become victims of their own success. 'They thought they'd entered the history books and in fact, they've never done anything remotely like it since; quite the contrary,' he said.

Maturana was more matter of fact, saying that the Argentina result had nothing to do with Colombia's performance the following summer. Had *Los Cafeteros* simply hit their peak in Buenos Aires meaning there was only one way to go? Injuries and a drop in form shattered Colombia's fragile confidence but Maturana was sure that if the World Cup had been played two months after the Argentina game, they would have won it. The Argentina win had raised expectations and failure from that point on would not be tolerated. By the time the dust had settled, Colombia had crashed out of the World Cup and a star defender lay in a Medellín morgue.

In his final column for Bogotá's *El Tiempo* newspaper, Escobar spoke of how Colombia could recover from the World Cup debacle, words that took on added meaning only days later: 'Life doesn't end here. We have to go on. Life cannot end here. No matter how difficult, we must stand back up. We only have two options: either allow anger to paralyse us and the violence continues, or we overcome and try our best to help others. It is our choice. Let us please maintain respect. My warmest regards to everyone. It has been the most amazing and rare experience. We'll see each other again soon because life does not end here.'

Colombia qualified for France 98 but an era had come to an end. A new, vibrant Colombia side managed by Argentine José Pékerman qualified for the 2014 World Cup and, powered by the goals of tournament top scorer James Rodríguez, made the quarter-finals in Brazil before exiting to the hosts.

The legacy of the Colombian players from the so-called Narco-Soccer era continues to this day. 'They put Colombia on the map, changed how Colombians saw their national team and created some of the country's first iconic players,' stated Worswick. 'Across the world now, ask anyone to name a Colombian and chances are Valderrama, Asprilla or Higuita would be the first names mentioned.'

Despite the tragedies and controversies these players gave hope to everyday Colombians during those dark, uncertain times of the 80s and 90s.

Chapter Twelve

God is Bulgarian

THE SUMMER of 1994 left an indelible imprint on Bulgarian football, one that remains more than two decades later. Bulgaria's World Cup record up to this point was miserable – played 12, won none, drawn four and lost eight. If it wasn't for two 'sliding doors' moments the events at USA 94 may never have happened at all.

Whenever Bulgaria's two premier sides (Levski Sofia and CSKA Sofia) met, tensions were high, but during the 1985 domestic cup final, they reached boiling point. Following several contentious refereeing decisions, a huge mêlée ensued which saw two players sent off. Sanctions were brought after the match which saw both Hristo Stoichkov and national goalkeeper Borislav Mikhailov banned for life, the latter for striking an official.

However, with the 1986 World Cup looming and Bulgaria making their first appearance in 12 years, the Bulgarian Football Union (BFS) feared humiliation on the game's biggest stage without their key players. They granted pardons to the players meaning Mikhailov and Stoichkov's playing careers were saved. Mikhailov was selected for Mexico 86 but the 20-year-old Stoichkov missed out and would have to bide his time to hit the world stage. Two defeats out of three continued Bulgaria's miserable World Cup run. Qualification for Italia 90 didn't go much better with Bulgaria finishing bottom of a four-team group, followed by a dismal showing in the Euro 92 qualifiers. There was no sign of what was about to transpire as the qualifying campaign for USA 94 began in earnest. Bulgaria were picked from pot four and placed in a group with France, Austria and Sweden.

Once a government sanction on players moving abroad was lifted, Stoichkov joined Johann Cruyff's Barcelona 'Dream Team'. He had scored an impressive 38 goals in 30 games for CSKA, convincing Cruyff to take him to Camp Nou where he won four league titles and formed a feared strike partnership with Brazil's Romário. Elsewhere, Yordan Letchkov and Petar Hubchev played for Bundesliga sides whilst gifted midfielder Krasimir Balakov and striker Emil Kostadinov were in Portugal with Sporting CP and Porto respectively.

Bulgaria's early qualifying campaign had something of a Jekyll-and-Hyde feel to it. Victories over Finland and France were tempered by reverses to Austria and Sweden; however two disappointing home draws with Israel and Sweden left qualification very much in the balance. Hopes were raised with an impressive 4-1 demolition of Austria in Sofia on the same night Israel shocked France which meant Bulgaria's slim chances rested on them repeating the trick against *Les Bleus* the following month.

When Eric Cantona met a Jean-Pierre Papin header to volley France into the lead after 31 minutes it looked as though the Israel game was out of their system. However, within six minutes Bulgaria brought themselves level when a Balakov corner picked Kostadinov out in a crowded penalty area. The mulleted hitman strained every sinew in his neck to power a header beyond Bernard Lama in the French goal.

A draw was still enough for the French, but they found themselves in the unenviable position of playing for the point knowing that another Bulgarian sucker punch would put paid to their World Cup chances. France manager Gérard Houllier replaced striker Papin with the mercurial winger David Ginola on 68 minutes, hardly a substitution to shore things up defensively.

With time almost up, France won a free kick wide on the right, deep in Bulgarian territory. The ball was played short to Ginola with all 48,000 fans in attendance expecting the coiffured winger to head for the corner flag to while away the final seconds. Perhaps annoyed at his benching after scoring in the Israel game, Ginola had other ideas and lifted a high cross towards Cantona, the lone Frenchman in the Bulgarian 18-yard box.

However, the cross sailed over Cantona's head and was rescued by Bulgarian full-back Emil Kremenliev. With the full-time whistle only seconds away, the Levski Sofia man and his team-mates poured forward as France scrambled back. The ball found Lyuboslav Penev, his deftly chipped pass fell into Kostadinov's stride and he cut inside his man before unleashing a shot past Lama.

Ninety minutes were up. Kostadinov raced away evading his jubilant team-mates before sinking to his knees. Bulgarian commentator Nikolay Kolev roared 'God is Bulgarian' into his microphone. The improbable had happened. Bulgaria were going to the World Cup at France's expense and Houllier never did forgive Ginola for his errant pass. Years later Ginola threatened legal action against his former manager after Houllier made derogatory remarks against him in his autobiography.

Bulgarian midfielder Zlatko Yankov had his own story to tell regarding the match, saying that the two men involved in the winning goal, Kostadinov and Penev, had entered France illegally. Both failed to secure visas and, allegedly with the help of Mikhailov and Georgi Georgiev, were smuggled into the country. According to Yankov, a low-security checkpoint was pin-pointed and the two men were whisked through before being transported to Paris where they joined up with the rest of the squad.

Having missed out on the previous two World Cups, a now 28-year-old Stoichkov would finally make his bow having helped Barcelona secure their fourth consecutive league title just a month earlier. Festivities were tempered, however, when the Spanish giants were humbled in a 4-0 defeat to Fabio Capello's AC Milan in the Champions League Final.

The exodus of players from Bulgaria had been detrimental to the standard of the domestic league but when manager Dimitar Penev named his 22-man World Cup squad, nine still played at home, predominantly with Levski Sofia. Namesake Lyuboslav missed out on selection as he underwent treatment for testicular cancer, having been diagnosed early in 1994. They would possess the drive of Balakov and Letchkov in midfield with Trifon Ivanov in defence ahead of the erstwhile Mikhailov. Up front the hardworking Kostadinov would provide the perfect foil for key man Stoichkov.

Bulgaria were grouped with World Cup debutants Nigeria, fellow Europeans Greece and one of the pre-tournament favourites, Argentina. With the South Americans widely expected to top Group D, second place was up for grabs. Despite Bulgaria's terrible World Cup record, the format – with three points for a win and places for four of the best third-placed sides in the knockout phase – meant there had never been a better chance to progress in a tournament.

'To be honest, we did not have a lot of pressure as expectations were low,' said Levski Sofia full-back Tsanko Tsvetanov. 'We were expected to get our first win and we were confident as we had players from the top European teams [in the squad]. Even more, my Levski team-mates and I had recently won a friendly game with Bayern Munich so we had enough confidence.'

Nigeria appeared to be something of an unknown quantity and had struggled against European opposition in the build-up, but any hopes of Bulgaria getting off to a dream start were dashed by the Super Eagles whose clinical ability in front of goal blew Penev's men away. Stoichkov had been limited in training; a strained thigh muscle had even put his selection in the balance.

Star striker Rashidi Yekini had been missing from the warm-up games and his first goal at the Cotton Bowl gave the Super Eagles a platform from which they put Bulgaria to the sword. The best Bulgaria could offer was a free kick from Stoichkov which found the net only for his effort to be ruled out as he had failed to spot that the referee had awarded an indirect free kick. Daniel Amokachi and Emmanuel Amunike added two more goals to complete a 3-0 win.

After the match both Penev and Stoichkov claimed they had failed to see a clear signal from the referee. The manager explained his frustrations to the *New York Times*: 'The team lost its motivation after the second goal and the quality of the game came down.' There was much work to be done ahead of the crucial second game with Greece at Chicago's Soldier Field, in front of a partisan *Ethniki-*

supporting crowd since the Windy City was home to large numbers of Greek immigrants.

The heavy defeat against Nigeria suggested Bulgaria would have their work cut out if they were to break their World Cup duck. Penev called a squad meeting and, to help release the tension, allowed the players to spend time with their partners at the team hotel. Penev only made one change to his starting XI: Levski's Nasko Sirakov replaced Daniel Borimirov, who had been substituted in the Nigeria game.

It was a must win for both teams, Greece having been hit for four by Argentina in their opening game. This was the Greeks' first World Cup appearance, having qualified from a group including Hungary, Russia and Yugoslavia. Alketas Panagoulias's side benefitted from Yugoslavia's FIFA suspension due to United Nations sanctions. As a reward for qualification Panagoulias had named a veteran squad, ignoring some of the impressive young talent the country was producing. The plan had backfired spectacularly in the first game with the *Ethniki* being seriously outclassed by Argentina.

Soldier Field could have been mistaken for a little corner of Greece with the stadium bedecked in blue-and-white flags of the ancient nation. Greek symbols adorned banners and the national anthem was belted out with gusto from the thousands of supporters. Several hundred Bulgarian fans huddled in the stands near the halfway line desperately trying to generate some noise to match that of their opponents.

They didn't have long to wait for the first goal. A lofted Balakov free kick ballooned into the penalty area and on to the head of Kostadinov. Defender Alexis Alexoudis fell under the challenge and batted the ball away with his arm as he landed on top of it leaving referee Ali Bujsaim no option but to point to the spot. Stoichkov despatched it with ease, sending AEK Athens goalkeeper Ilias Atmatsidis – one of six new players called upon after the Nigeria debacle – the wrong way in the process.

Bulgaria were good value for their lead but failed to add a second in the first half. Balakov shot over after a less-than-graceful attempt at gathering a cross by Atmatsidis, but a second goal seemed to be only a matter of time. Greece had chances, albeit half ones; a long-range effort was comfortably saved by Mikhailov and a weak header was sent wide. Ultimately their attacks were too slow and Panagoulias's men lacked a real cutting edge up front.

Ten minutes into the second half Bulgaria again caught Greece napping with a lofted free kick. Sirakov attempted to race clear of the defence only to be halted by Ioannis Kalitzakis who sent him sprawling into a 50/50 challenge with Atmatsidis. As defenders attempted to clear the ball, Sirakov got back to his feet only for the Greek goalkeeper to haul him back to the ground. Bujsaim didn't need much persuading to blow his whistle and Bulgaria were awarded their second penalty. This time, Atmatsidis guessed right but the precision of Stoichkov secured both his and Bulgaria's second goal.

Letchkov was next on the scoresheet, getting on the end of a neat one-two that sliced the Greek defence in half. The number nine, whose physical appearance belied his 26 years, slotted home, the ball glancing the post on its way into the net. The rout was completed in injury time when Stoichkov, on a hat-trick, tried his luck with a free kick from distance. Atmatsidis got his hand to the shot but could only send the ball spinning back towards goal where substitute Daniel Borimirov gobbled up the rebound.

Bulgaria had bounced back from the disappointment of the Nigeria defeat and could have easily scored more than four. Referee Bujsaim had threatened to ruin the game as a spectacle with his card-happy approach, cautioning eight players, four from either side. The small pocket of Bulgarian supporters roared their approval blowing trumpets and inexplicably a set of bagpipes as they finally celebrated their country's first World Cup win, at the 18th attempt.

In Group D's final game at the Cotton Bowl, Bulgaria were boosted by the news of Maradona's tournament exit as Penev named the same starting XI that had thrashed Greece.

Just as in Chicago, the Bulgarian fans were dwarfed by the amount of opposition support in attendance. Penev looked to nullify the Argentines, hoping one point would be enough for qualification. This Argentina were a different prospect to the one from the tournament's first two games, Basile going as far as to admit after the game that the loss of Maradona had affected his players. The Argentinians were in shock and played like it, Bulgaria were primed and ready to take advantage of it.

Defenders Hubchev and Ivanov were more than a match for anything the Argentine attackers threw their way. Ivanov in particular had impressed with his performances and had also gained something of a cult following due partly to his style of play and his somewhat intimidating appearance. The defender known to team-mates as *Tunyo* was something of an anomaly in the Bulgarian squad as he mixed happily with the CSKA faction (led by Stoichkov) and the Levski camp (headed by Mikhailov).

Ivanov had anchored the defence that kept the Argentine threat at bay reducing them to long-range efforts in the first half whilst Kostadinov saw a headed effort ruled out for offside. Shortly after the hour mark, Stoichkov sprung the offside trap to give Bulgaria the lead. A quick, incisive counter-attack saw Kostadinov release the Bulgarian hitman with a perfectly weighted pass that the Barcelona man stabbed past Luis Islas to make it 1-0.

Six minutes later, Bulgaria were reduced to ten men when Tsanko Tsvetanov picked up a second yellow card, two of nine issued in the match by Tunisian referee Neji Jouini. Despite being a man down, the Bulgarian defence were resolute. Substitute Ramón Medina Bello spurned *La Albiceleste*'s best chance whilst their passing became more erratic as the game went on. Balakov almost added a second in the 86th minute but Islas managed to tip his effort over the bar.

With time ticking away, Argentina became more desperate. Strikers Balbo and Batistuta failed to find the net before an unmarked Sirakov rose to head a Balakov corner past Islas in injury time to cap Bulgaria's second win. Bulgaria, Argentina and Nigeria all finished on six points; the Nigerians topped Group D with a slightly superior goal difference. Thanks to the win in Dallas, Bulgaria were second with Argentina having to settle for one of the best third-place berths.

After the opening defeat to Nigeria, the Bulgarian defence had stood firm in its next two games, keeping clean sheets in both. Further progression now though would hinge on how the usually settled side would cope without three of their regular line-up. Defenders Ivanov, Tsvetanov and midfielder Yankov were all suspended for the first knockout stage having felt the wrath of the strict Jouini in the Argentina game.

Mexico were Bulgaria's next opponent at Giants Stadium, having won Group E ahead of Italy, Ireland and Norway. Cocksure captain Jorge Campos told the *New York Times*,

'We've come through the toughest group, why shouldn't we go all the way to the final?' Both teams fancied their chances and knew they were more than capable of securing a quarter-final berth. Mexico's hopes lay with the flamboyant Campos, winger Luis 'Zague' Alves and Atlético Madrid midfielder Luis García whose two goals against Ireland had built the platform for *El Tri*'s progress.

The counter-attacking system that had caught Argentina out in Dallas was in full effect at the Meadowlands. Stoichkov was again released ahead of the defence with an incisive pass, he took one touch before rifling a shot past the neon-shirted Campos in the Mexico goal. Bulgaria's makeshift defence surrendered the lead 12 minutes later when Emil Kremenliev felled Zague in the box. The Mexican attacker was giving the Levski Sofia man a torrid time: Kremenliev's had been the first name to go into referee Al-Sharif's notebook for a cynical foul a few minutes earlier.

Alberto García Aspe stepped up and sent Mikhailov the wrong way to level the game. Hindered by another fussy referee eager to issue cards, the game became disjointed. Kremenliev was sent off for two yellow cards shortly after half-time but Mexico failed to take advantage as dangerman Luis García suffered the same fate eight minutes later. A rather turgid game crawled towards its conclusion, interspersed with Al-Sharif's card display and the goal collapsing after some Mexican defenders collided with it.

Campos and Mikhailov kept the scores level when called upon but with both sides reduced to ten men it seemed inevitable that the game would go to extra time. Penev made two changes during the extra 30 minutes, eager to introduce fresh legs into the side. His Mexican counterpart Miguel Mejía Barón inexplicably kept his substitutes on the bench for the whole 120 minutes, despite having two capable strikers to call upon.

With extra time unable to separate the two sides, USA 94 played host to its first penalty shoot-out. García Aspe stepped up first for *El Tri* but the composure he possessed earlier in the game to beat Mikhailov deserted him as he fired his effort high over the bar. Advantage Bulgaria, but then the usually dependable Balakov could only find the fluorescent sleeves of Campos with his effort. Midfielder Marcelino Bernal stepped up second for Mexico and suffered the same fate as the previous two takers. Three penalties, three misses.

The first of Penev's substitutes, Bontcho Guentchev, who played in England with Ipswich Town, put the American spectators out of their misery with a fine drive down the middle of Campos's goal to put Bulgaria ahead in the best of five. Jorge Rodríguez struck Mexico's next spot kick the opposite side to Bernal's, but Mikhailov guessed right again to keep it out. When Borimirov made it 2-0, Claudio Suárez had to score his penalty, or the game was over.

The defender succeeded and passed the responsibility back to the Bulgarians and Letchkov, who was named as the fourth penalty taker. The Hamburg man strode forward confidently and side-footed a rising shot high into the top corner out of the reach of Campos. After more than two hours, the game was over.

Campos lay face down with arms outstretched for a full two minutes in the Giants Stadium penalty area whilst Bulgaria celebrated. Stoichkov, who had been front and centre of the Bulgarian effort thus far, was scheduled to take the fifth penalty but for once he was not needed. 'God was Bulgarian today,' he told the press afterwards, but years later he claimed a mole in the Mexico set-up had revealed tactics and more to him beforehand. With the reigning champions up next, maybe more divine intervention would be required.

The quarter-final tie with Germany saw Bulgaria remain at Giants Stadium and Penev gave his charges the day off to celebrate long into the night at the team hotel in Princeton, New Jersey. The players' request to leave the secluded hotel and move closer to Manhattan fell on deaf ears with BFS officials as the fragile peace between the two factions threatened to shatter. The Bulgarian players managed to relax though as they celebrated Letchkov and Penev's birthday the day before the game. An FBI detail who shadowed the squad were amazed to find them laughing, drinking and smoking before the biggest game of their lives.

Usually, the prospect of playing Germany in a major football tournament would give opponents sleepless nights but the unassuming Bulgarians refused to be intimidated, having become accustomed to their underdog role. Once again, the Bulgarian fans were heavily outnumbered in the stands where a total of 72,416 would be in attendance.

The stuttering Germans had failed to set the tournament alight thus far but had shown signs of improvement in their 3-2 win over Belgium in the previous round. *Die Mannschaft* were led by captain Lothar Matthäus and the goal threat of Jürgen Klinsmann. Bulgaria's movement and pace caused their supposed superior opponents problems in the early exchanges. Sirakov stung the palms of Bodo Illgner in the Germany goal, having been set up by Letchkov who then played in Stoichkov from a short free kick, his cut-back fired against the post by Balakov.

At the other end Klinsmann had the best of Germany's chances, first with a free header straight at Mikhailov before he sliced a shot wide. German midfielder Andreas Möller looked certain to score shortly before the break only for his strike to hit Ivanov between the legs, the brave defender felled by the effort. Both sides had traded chances but the game remained level at the break. Bulgaria looked more than capable of causing the reigning champions problems.

Three minutes after the restart, however, the deadlock was broken. A raking high ball into the penalty area by Martin Wagner found Klinsmann who, sensing a challenge from Letchkov, knocked the ball inside his opponent. Letchkov brushed the striker's knee and, never one to need much of an invitation to hit the ground, Klinsmann was felled. Despite Letchkov's protestations, Mexican referee José Torres Cadena awarded a penalty. The ever-dependable Matthäus coolly despatched the resulting spot kick.

Sensing blood, the Germans almost immediately put the game out of reach. Möller rocketed a shot against the upright with Rudi Völler's follow-up denied by the linesman's flag. The let-off sparked the Bulgarian attack into life, as Stoichkov was bundled to the ground by Möller on 75 minutes, 25 yards from Illgner's goal.

The Barcelona striker dusted himself off and spun the ball several times before placing it on the turf. Balakov stood nearby but the focused look on Stoichkov's face suggested that he would be taking the free kick. His team-mate moved away, leaving Stoichkov standing almost horizontal to the ball. Three steps were all he needed to whip a curling shot over the German wall and into the vast Giants Stadium net, leaving Illgner merely a bystander.

Stoichkov raced away punching the air before looking skyward and crossing himself. The small section of Bulgarian fans in the stands were in rapture, waving flags as Stoichkov's team-mates caught up with him to celebrate. Bulgarian tails were up and, before Germany could regroup, Kostadinov won a corner after a brisk counter-attack.

Germany failed to clear their lines conceding a throw-in from Balakov's corner. A hint of a foul throw was ignored by Cadena and the ball found Yankov in the right channel. A quick look up from the Levski man saw an obvious mismatch in the penalty area where the diminutive Thomas Häßler had been left to mark the towering Letchkov. Yankov's clipped cross was inch-perfect, Letchkov darted inside his marker and met the ball fully with his balding pate. Häßler stood no chance and an outstretched Illgner could do nothing as Letchkov's header spun out of his reach. Within three minutes the game had been turned on its head.

Later Penev revealed he was ready to substitute both Stoichkov and Sirakov moments before the equaliser, a decision which cost the Germans their place in the tournament and secured Bulgaria an unlikely place in the semi-finals. Stoichkov's goal was made even sweeter as he dedicated it to his daughter Mihaela who turned six years old that day. 'We had great belief; it wasn't the first time we had done this, we did the same in Paris,' said Tsvetanov remembering the memorable qualifier with France.

The victory in New Jersey was the pinnacle of Bulgarian football, they had defeated Germany and had gone from having no World Cup wins to being one game away from the final. They remained at Giants Stadium where Italy awaited. It proved to be one game too far as the *Azzurri*, backed by Roberto Baggio, defeated the plucky Bulgarians 2-1. Stoichkov did manage to add another goal to his tally, joining Russia's Oleg Salenko as the tournament's joint top goalscorer with six.

Stoichkov had filled the rest of the squad with enough confidence to convince them they could win the tournament but the striker exited with an unspecified leg injury in the second half. Speaking to the press afterwards, Stoichkov bemoaned the performance of referee Joel Quiniou; harking back to the decisive qualifier back in Paris the previous November, Stoichkov quipped that 'God was still on our side, but the referee was French.' Tsvetanov too felt the Bulgarians were hard done by when it came to the match official's decisions: 'Maybe if there was VAR (Video Assistant Referee) at the time we would have made the final.'

There was almost a sense of inevitability about the third-place play-off defeat to Sweden. The 4-0 thumping did little to detract from a Bulgaria side who had to fly 3,000 miles to Pasadena's Rose Bowl for the game, having also had a day's less rest than their opponents. This perhaps explained that having conceded seven goals in their previous six games they managed to let in the same amount during 31 first-half minutes against Sweden.

The sheer scale of Bulgaria's achievements at USA 94 was emphasised four years later when they returned to the World Cup in France. Normal service resumed as they drew one and lost two of their three games before being eliminated at the group stages. Some of the rag-tag bunch had become household names, noticeably Ivanov, Stoichkov plus the follicly challenged Letchkov and Mikhailov.

The tragic death of Ivanov to a heart attack in 2016 brought back memories of that famous side. Bulgaria have not made a World Cup since that group disbanded and it remains to be seen whether the south-eastern European country will produce the likes of it ever again.

Chapter Thirteen

The Class of 94

SWEDEN'S BEST World Cup finish came on home soil in 1958 when they defeated Hungary, Mexico, the Soviet Union and West Germany on the way to qualifying for their first final. Unfortunately for the *Blågult*, they ran into a Brazil side inspired by a 17-year-old Pelé in the final and lost 5-2. When, during the Covid-19 pandemic, Swedish broadcaster SVT looked through its archives for something to 'strengthen and unite' the country, it looked past the exploits of the team led by Englishman George Raynor. Instead, it treated the nation to the performances of the 'Class of 94', Sweden's greatest ever national side.

That seemed most unlikely back in 1990, when Sweden qualified for their first World Cup since 1978 but found Italia 90 to be a disaster. They lost all three group games 2-1 including an embarrassing defeat to Bora Milutinović's Costa Rica which put an exclamation point on the miserable campaign. Olle Nordin was out as manager, replaced by Tommy Svensson, who had taken Tromsø to two top-three finishes in the Norwegian first division.

The impact of Svensson's appointment was immediate. Sweden once again flourished in a tournament they hosted as they came within a game of making the 1992 European Championships Final. At the same stadium in Solna where Brazil vanquished them in 1958, it was Germany who broke Swedish hearts this time, with a 3-2 win ending the hopes of an all-Scandinavian final with Denmark. 'Euro 92 was the beginning of the good times for Swedish football,' remembered goalkeeper Thomas Ravelli. 'We beat England in Stockholm and had also learnt how to prepare for tournaments, when to practice, when to rest, what to eat etc.'

The goalkeeper's loud persona on the pitch had seen him gain something of a madcap reputation, similar to many who play his position. Over the years, team-mates spoke of occasions where they arrived in the changing rooms only to find their trousers cut to shreds. At this stage in his career, Ravelli had eschewed the chance to join his countrymen abroad by staying in Sweden, firstly, with Östers IF, where he won two Allsvenskan titles, latterly with IFK Göteborg, where he would add a further five titles.

Sweden's star man at the time was 22-year-old baby-faced attacker Tomas Brolin, who burst on to the international scene to lead the line for his country at Italia 90. Despite the team's underwhelming effort his own performances had not gone unrecognised; he joined Italian side Parma for £1.2m and was awarded the *Guldbollen* as Sweden's footballer of the year.

Two years later, Brolin again was the key man for the *Blågult*, ending the European Championships as joint top scorer with three goals. By the time the 1994 World Cup qualifying campaign began, Brolin had been joined in Europe by several of his international team-mates. Strike partner Martin Dahlin was in Germany with Borussia Mönchengladbach, midfielders Stefan Schwarz and captain Jonas Thern were at Benfica and Napoli respectively, whilst beanpole hitman Kennet Andersson was at Lille in Ligue 1.

Qualification for USA 94 came easily for Sweden and unlike group opponents France and Bulgaria they avoided any late drama, suffering only one defeat in their ten games. The previous tournament's travails had given the Swedish players a close bond. When Svensson named his 22-man squad, the overseas contingent was supplemented by a core of ten domestic-based players, seven of which played for IFK Göteborg, including the manager's nephew, Joachim Björklund.

Sweden had been placed in a group with favourites Brazil, Italia 90 surprise package Cameroon and Russia, playing in their first tournament as an independent nation. If a diverse group of opponents wasn't enough for the Swedes to contend with, the games would be played in the Rose Bowl's California sunshine and the oppressive greenhouse humidity of Michigan's Pontiac Silverdome.

The Swedish FA (SvFF), eager to improve on the results at Italia 90, sent a team to scout training bases and left no stone unturned in improving the national team's chances. 'We had physicians and doctors to help us acclimatise to the heat and even took our own chef,' said Ravelli. 'We were told how to play in the heat, when to rest and even how much to drink.'

Ravelli's international career had begun in 1981 but by the summer of 1994 the 34-year-old's selection had come under question by the Swedish football press. They pondered whether his inclusion was merely down to a lack of competition but Svensson was unmoved, putting his faith in the man who had donned the gloves in Sweden's previous two tournaments. 'There were no expectations, the press didn't expect us to get through the group,' said Ravelli. 'We lost 1-0 to Denmark in Copenhagen and the press blamed me for the goal, saying I was too old now and not good enough.'

The kick-off time for the opening game was 4.30pm when temperatures would be around 33°C. Svensson opted for a 4-4-2 formation with Brolin chosen to partner Dahlin up front ahead of Andersson and young Feyenoord striker Henrik Larsson. A packed Rose Bowl hoped to catch a glimpse of the Indomitable Lions' 1990 World Cup hero Roger Milla but were disappointed to see the 42-year-old striker on the bench.

Any Swedish misgivings over the temperatures seemed unfounded when, in the eighth minute, defender Roger Ljung headed in a deep Jonas Thern free kick to give his side an early lead. Cameroon, the first African side to reach the World Cup quarter-finals back in 1990, responded quickly as Swedish defender Patrick Andersson had an afternoon to forget.

Played into trouble by a team-mate, Andersson's attempted clearance smacked off Marc-Vivien Foé, who was now in on goal. Drawing Ravelli out, the Cameroon midfielder rolled the ball across to David Embé who got ahead of his marker to equalise. The Swedish defence appealed for offside but Trinidadian linesman Douglas James remained unmoved as Embé danced by the corner flag.

After the first goal, Sweden had allowed Cameroon back into the game whilst the Africans restricted their European opponents to a few long-range efforts. The game was evenly poised as both teams emerged from the shadows to begin the second half. Two minutes after the restart a throw-in on the left found its way to Cameroon full-back Rigobert Song.

The former Liverpool man was allowed time to look up and launch a long ball towards François Omam-Biyick, who was being marshalled by two defenders. Patrick Andersson lost track of the flight of the ball as it dropped over his head to Omam-Biyick, scorer of Cameroon's famous winner against Argentina at Italia 90, who ran on and stabbed the ball past Ravelli to give the Indomitable Lions what had seemed an unlikely lead.

With an hour gone, Svensson had seen enough. He replaced right-winger Jesper Blomqvist with Larsson and switched Brolin out to the flank. Dahlin had caused Cameroon plenty of problems all afternoon, winning the free kick for Ljung's goal, but had also spurned a hatful of chances that were threatening to haunt the Swedes. The Cameroon defence was visibly wilting though and Dahlin thought he had found the equaliser only for it to be ruled out for handball.

As the Indomitable Lions' defence dropped deeper and deeper, they now had a dreadlocked 22-year-old running at them in the shape of Larsson. He received the ball and, with few other options available, sent a ferocious swerving 35-yard shot at goal. The ball dipped over Cameroon's stricken goalkeeper Joseph-Antoine Bell's head and crashed against the crossbar. The ball bounced down where Dahlin waited. He controlled the rebound on his chest before lashing the ball into the cavernous Rose Bowl net. The oft-mentioned heat had taken its toll on both sets of players and the game petered out into a 2-2 draw.

Sweden had a point on the board, one more than they had managed from three games at Italia 90. 'We lost three games 2-1 at Italia 90 so to get a point and not lose again was unbelievably important. It would have seen a lot of negativity from the press and damaged confidence,' said Ravelli.

Up next were Russia, who had lost 2-0 to Brazil in their opening game. On paper, they should have been heading to the USA with one of the strongest squads at the World Cup. Since sealing qualification, however, they had suffered internal problems that ended with 14 players signing a letter asking for the removal of coach Pavel Sadyrin.

Unhappy with his methods as well as issues within the Russian Football Union, they stated that unless changes were made, they would not play for their country at the World Cup. A charm offensive ensued with eight of the 14 backing down and making themselves available. Amongst the half-dozen missing were stars Igor Shalimov, Sergei Kiryakov, Igor Kolyvanov and Andrei Kanchelskis.

Furious with the Brazil defeat, Sadyrin castigated his players in the press, a usual practice of his. The main focus of his ire was inexperienced defender Vladislav Ternavsky, who had the unenviable task of shackling Romário in the opening game. The diminutive Brazilian gave Ternavsky nightmares and Sadyrin responded by making five changes ahead of the Sweden game, the hapless defender being one of them.

For Sweden, Svensson brought in Andersson to partner Dahlin upfront, shifting a disgruntled Brolin out of his favoured free-attacking role to the right wing. Faced with defensive duties, Brolin was placated by the experienced Roland Nilsson who told him to concentrate on attacking and to leave the defending to him.

The new tactics weren't an immediate success. Roger Ljung was adjudged to have tripped Aleksandr Borodyuk in the penalty area. Logroñés striker Oleg Salenko stepped up to convert from the spot to give Russia the lead. Knowing another defeat would all but result in Russia's exit from the tournament, Sadyrin decided to try to sit on the lead, as goalkeeper Dmitri Kharine of Chelsea was inexplicably booked for time-wasting after only 34 minutes.

As whistles and boos reverberated around the Silverdome in response to Russia's questionable strategy, Brolin brought Sweden level. Kennet Andersson used all his 6ft 4in frame to hold the ball up in Russian territory, hooking it over his head towards the ever-dangerous Dahlin. Referee Joël Quiniou was unhappy with the close attention defender Sergei Gorlukovich was paying the Swedish striker and pointed to the spot. Brolin stepped up and fired past Kharine to bring the *Blågult* level.

Gorlukovich had been treading a disciplinary tightrope since being booked in the first minute. A further transgression on Dahlin five minutes after the break saw Quiniou issue him with a second yellow card that reduced Russia to ten men. However, Dahlin was also too carpeted by the strict Frenchman and received his second booking of the tournament, meaning he would be suspended for the final group game with Brazil. Sweden were now on top with Russia chasing shadows, Gorlukovich's sending off making their task even more arduous.

The breakthrough came on the hour mark as Dahlin headed home a Thern cross. Sweden were well in the ascendancy now and, with the Russians physically spent, Dahlin scored another header eight minutes from time. Kennet Andersson was the supplier and Svensson's plan to pair the two up front and drop Brolin deeper ultimately proved to be an inspired one. Another tactical masterclass would be needed for the final group game as Dahlin's impending suspension posed a conundrum for Svensson.

Sadyrin refused to speak to the media after the game, sending his assistant to answer questions including why he dropped dangerman Sergei Yuran for the game. Sadyrin's nightmare did seem to be coming to an end, however, with sources suggesting he would either resign or be replaced as Russia coach following their second defeat.

With Dahlin suspended, Svensson brought Larsson into the starting XI for the Brazil game, which again would be played at the Pontiac Silverdome. Brazil had played their first two games at Palo Alto's Stanford Stadium so moving to the Silverdome would require some adjustments for Carlos Alberto Parreira's men. Not only would it be the first time *O Seleção* had played a competitive game indoors, but the pitch was also both seven feet shorter and narrower than the one they were accustomed to.

Brazil had hammered Cameroon 3-0 in their second group game, Romário again on the scoresheet. Svensson knew you had to stop the Diabolical Duo of Bebeto and Romário if you stood any chance of defeating Brazil. Having noticed how ineffective the man-to-man marking deployed by Russia and Cameroon had been, Svensson didn't want the responsibility to rest on one player's shoulders and opted for a zonal defence.

Added to the defensive strategy was also a change in Sweden's overall tactics. They were less attack-minded than in previous games and the patient approach seemed to pay dividends when Kennet Andersson gave them the lead. Brolin rode a challenge from Aldair before a sumptuous pass found the Lille striker on the left edge of the Brazilian 18-yard box. Andersson controlled the ball on his chest before stretching a telescopic leg to poke the ball high over Taffarel and into the Brazil goal.

In the group's other game, at Stanford Stadium, Russia were playing with the freedom of a team heading out of the tournament and had a 3-0 half-time lead over Cameroon. Qualification was all but secured for the sides at the

Silverdome as the second half began. Romário burst through the defence and again displayed his penchant for shooting whenever the goalkeeper least expected it. A swift poke of his right foot sent the ball bobbling past Ravelli for his third World Cup goal and levelled the scores.

Meanwhile the score in Palo Alto had spiralled out of control. Oleg Salenko had placed himself firmly at the top of the goalscoring charts by scoring an unfathomable five goals in the 6-1 rout. In a game of records, Roger Milla became the oldest player to score in the World Cup when he scored a mere consolation two minutes into the second half.

With the Brazil game ending 1-1, Sweden finished the group stage unbeaten on five points and in the process also managed to avoid meeting the Dutch in the first knockout round. 'We could have won the game,' insisted Ravelli. 'Brazil were very similar to us, playing 4-4-2 and were more of a team than a collection of technical players.'

Saudi Arabia awaited in Texas on the following Sunday afternoon. Svensson decided that a short passing game would be the order of the day with attacks launched only when necessary. 'The heat in Los Angeles wasn't too bad but Dallas was by far the toughest with temperatures between 40 and 50°C in the sun,' said Ravelli.

Dahlin was back up front as Svensson again relied on the same core of players that had got them this far. Sweden's softly, softly approach resulted in an early goal as Kennet Andersson and Dahlin combined once more. Andersson received the ball in his usual position before a sharp turn gave him enough room to whip a cross towards the back post. Dahlin, quick as a flash, held his run until Andersson made contact, losing his marker and heading the ball low between Saudi goalkeeper Mohammed Al-Deayea and the far post.

With the lead, Sweden became compact and refused to chase Jorge Solari's side around the vast Cotton Bowl pitch. Previously Saudi Arabia had surprised teams with their exceptional movement and incisive passing but Sweden appeared to be the first team to have done any homework on them. Andersson added a second goal on 50 minutes, Brolin again the protagonist, picking out the lanky striker with a long pass. With skills usually uncommon for a player of his size, Andersson chipped the ball over his incoming marker before firing a low left-footed drive from the edge of the area across goal and past Al-Deayea. Andersson raced away before performing his iconic celebration, a carbon copy of an Australian Rules Football referee awarding a goal.

Saudi Arabia enjoyed a brief ten-minute spell before the game was again reduced to walking pace in the final minutes. Solari's men injected some life into the final proceedings when Fahad Al-Ghesheyan cut inside the defence before unleashing a ferocious shot that gave Ravelli no chance. Any hopes of a comeback were extinguished, however, when, following a short, sharp link-up between Brolin, Dahlin and Andersson, the last of these fired home his second to put the game out of the Green Falcons' reach. Sweden were once again precise and efficient, scoring three excellent goals to set up a quarter-final clash with another European side exceeding all expectations, Romania.

Until this stage in the competition, Sweden's success had been down to the attacking threat of Brolin, Dahlin and Andersson. Defensively Sweden had yet to keep a clean sheet though; despite the mishaps against Cameroon in the group opener, they had shown resilience when faced with Bebeto and Romário.

During the Romania match, Sweden's tactics again worked to perfection. Svensson realised the best way to nullify a counter-attacking side like the Romanians was not to attack them in the first place. This did, however, lead to a drab encounter which suddenly sprang to life on 78 minutes with a goal straight from the training ground. Sweden had won a free kick some 30 yards from goal, with Schwarz and Mild standing over the ball. Schwarz feigned to strike the ball but left it for Mild who slotted a pass down the side of the six-man defensive wall. Brolin had positioned himself inches behind the Romanians and darted towards Mild's pass before unleashing a shot across Florin Prunea and into the far corner of the net.

With time running out for Romania, the talents of captain Gheorghe Hagi came to the fore. First, he tested Ravelli with a free kick from distance, then came a second bite at the apple when another free kick was awarded from a near-identical position. This time Hagi played a one-two with Dumitrescu before rifling a shot into the Swedish wall. The ball ricocheted into the path of Florin Răducioiu who couldn't miss and the game was headed to extra time.

It would be Răducioiu again who gave Romania the lead in the final 30 minutes with another strike that found its way to him via a Swedish boot. His second goal looked to be the winner, especially when midfielder Schwarz picked up a second yellow card a minute later that reduced Sweden to ten men.

Now Sweden had no choice but to push men forward. Captain Nilsson, usually resolute in his defensive duties, found himself inside the opposition half with the ball at his feet. With aching limbs and time running out he lofted a high ball towards the Romanian goal. Nilsson's punt appeared to be heading for the safe hands of Prunea but Andersson timed his jump to perfection as he leapt in front of the goalkeeper. With a swish of blond hair, his head met the ball to bring the scores level once more and send the game to a penalty shoot-out.

That day Ravelli had tied the Swedish record for most international appearances with 115. He would turn 35 the following month and the opportunity to make his 116th in a World Cup semi-final rested on his shoulders. Despite his status as the elder statesman of the Sweden squad, he was not averse to taking advice from less experienced team-mates. As the referee collated the names of the would-be takers, Brolin approached Ravelli to suggest he stand in the middle of the goal for as long as possible, giving no idea of which way he would dive. 'There wasn't preparation like you see today, you went more with a feeling and how the taker approached the ball,' remembered Ravelli. 'It's a lot easier for goalkeepers now, every game is televised and a goalkeeper coach with data on the percentage chance of where each kick would go.'

Proceedings didn't start well for the *Blågult* when Mild ballooned Sweden's first effort over the bar. The next six penalties found the net but still Ravelli stuck with the plan as Dan Petrescu made his way from the centre circle hoping to put Romania 4-3 ahead. Ravelli stared at the defender as he placed the ball on the spot. As before, the Swedish stopper waited until the final moment then sprang to his left as Petrescu struck the ball. The penalty was at the perfect height for Ravelli and he punched the ball away.

The scores were level as Ravelli waved his fist in celebration to team-mates at the halfway line, some of whom were so exhausted they could no longer stand. Two more penalties were converted and, with the score now 4-4, the shoot-out was headed for sudden death. Larsson was next knowing a miss could spell the end, but showed nerves of steel as he smashed his penalty beyond Prunea. Romania needed defender Miodrag Belodedici to score to keep their hopes alive. The accomplished defender hesitated as he prepared to take the kick. All cameras were trained on him. Ravelli swayed on the line, grabbing at his sweat-sodden shorts as they clung to his weary legs.

The penalty went the same way as Petrescu's effort, with hundreds of cameras in the stadium clicking away as Ravelli once more committed at the last second. The strike was further into the corner than Petrescu's but Ravelli plunged an outstretched arm towards it. With another strong fist, he beat the ball to safety and Sweden were in the semi-final of the World Cup for the first time since 1958. Larsson set off like a sprinter and was the first to greet Ravelli, jumping into his arms as the rest of the squad joined in. 'I had a good penalty record for Göteborg and Sweden. I had positive thoughts and a lot of confidence that I would be the hero,' the triumphant goalkeeper remembered.

Back in Sweden, the country was in rapture. Swedish newspaper *Aftonbladet* included a 16-page pull-out in the following day's edition, its headline reading 'Yes! This Was the Wildest Party of All.' News broke of a baby being delivered in Stockholm's central square as the mother-to-be was unable to get through the crowds to the hospital. Elsewhere, a man in Malmö suffered a heart attack during the game but refused to let his wife phone for an ambulance before it had finished.

You could have been forgiven for thinking Sweden had won the tournament, such was the euphoria across the nation. Sweden hadn't seen sporting success at this level since the 1970 heyday of tennis champion Björn Borg. As the sun came up in the morning, celebrations continued; cars honked their horns as revellers climbed up traffic lights and lampposts. However, the players would have to dust themselves down quickly as in less than three days they would be back at the Rose Bowl for a semi-final match-up with Brazil.

Sweden arrived in Pasadena as the walking wounded with four of Svensson's starters doubtful for the semi-final, whilst Schwarz was also suspended. Dahlin, who had missed the group game through suspension, had a nagging calf strain that had forced him off against Romania. Björklund and midfielder Klas Ingesson were also hampered with muscle injuries whilst Thern desperately tried to shake off a knee sprain that had kept him out of the quarter-final too. Meanwhile, Brazil had enjoyed an extra day's rest whilst also taking care of the Netherlands in 90 minutes, as opposed to Sweden needing 120 plus penalties to despatch Romania.

One area in which Sweden had an advantage over Brazil was in the height department; Kennet Andersson in particular had proved to be a very potent threat. The Swedes had been free-scoring so far. Dahlin too had found the net regularly with his head, but Brazil arguably boasted the premium strike duo at the World Cup in Romário and Bebeto. Their pace would not be welcomed by the drained Swedes.

The four doubtful players all recovered enough to take their place in Svensson's starting line-up as Sweden and Brazil continued their long-standing World Cup relationship. Ravelli made early saves from Branco and Romário as Brazil threatened to put their opponents to the sword during the early exchanges. Sweden defended deep, surrendering the flanks to the blue-shirted Brazilians, who kept Mauro Silva in the middle of the pitch to allow their full-backs free rein on the flanks.

Sweden were holding on, relying on muscle memory as the travails of the previous three weeks finally looked to have taken their toll. Matters worsened on 63 minutes when Colombian referee José Torres Cadena sent Thern off for a foul on Brazil captain Dunga. Thern accepted his punishment, shaking his Brazilian counterpart's hand before exiting the pitch. Svensson reacted by replacing an ineffective Dahlin with midfielder Stefan Rehn ahead of an expected Brazilian onslaught.

The resistance lasted 18 minutes. Jorginho received the ball wide right and with pinpoint accuracy found the head of Romário. Much of the talk beforehand had been of Sweden's height advantage but the 5ft 6in hitman got between two defenders to power a header past Ravelli and plunge a dagger into Swedish hearts. Throughout history, Brazil had been famed for their attacking flair but it was their suffocating defence that had provided the base for this performance. Parreira's Brazil was a more complete, practical unit that had restricted Sweden to three efforts on Taffarel's goal, minuscule when compared to Brazil's 26.

Sweden's journey was over, they struggled to overcome Brazil's tactical know-how and with Thern's dismissal their ability to turn defence into attack was extinguished. A comfortable 4-0 win over Bulgaria in the third-place play-off guaranteed Sweden a bronze medal and they were treated like champions upon their return home. An estimated 100,000 fans, including emergency workers, officials and even the prime minister were on hand as the Swedish squad arrived in a chartered plane escorted by fighter jets.

Sweden were the highest scorers at USA 94. Svensson's masterstroke decision to drop Brolin deeper to accommodate Andersson meant that the new strike partnership with Dahlin plundered more goals than even Brazil's forward line. 'We had players playing together at their top level, Brolin, Andersson, Dahlin, Schwarz and myself,' said Ravelli. 'A coach with World Cup experience as a player with a very intelligent assistant in Tord Grip. We had bench players who didn't complain and supported those who did [play].'

So-called 'golden generations' were plentiful at the 1994 World Cup but perhaps none has been so revered by its people as Sweden's 'Class of 94'.

Chapter Fourteen

Divine Intervention

DURING THE early 90s, Italian football had reached its zenith. Domestically, the world's greatest footballers had descended on the peninsula with Serie A widely viewed as the place to be. In 1994, AC Milan were reigning European champions. Playmaker Roberto Baggio was the current holder of the Ballon d'Or, the award for Europe's best footballer, and seemed a shoo-in to repeat the feat.

Internationally, the *Azzurri* had last won the World Cup in 1982 when Enzo Bearzot's side shocked the world by defeating Zico's Brazil on the way to a final victory over West Germany. Any hopes of a repeat were dashed with a second-round exit at Mexico 86 and the three-time champions looked to get back on track when they hosted the tournament four years later. Heroes were made in Salvatore Schillaci and the magisterial Baggio or *Il Divin Codino* ('the Divine Ponytail') and all was going to plan until the *Azzurri* faltered in the semi-finals as they lost to Argentina in a penalty shoot-out.

Bearzot's replacement Azeglio Vicini appeared to catch lightning in a bottle with Schillaci, although he would never hit the heights of Italia 90 again. Meanwhile, Baggio spent the next four years cultivating his reputation as the game's premier *trequartista*. In the two seasons leading up to Italia 90, Baggio had been in imperious form, despite Italy's fascination with defensive football. The World Cup win in 1982 had helped solidify the *catenaccio* style of play. Victory was built on a suffocating defence with a functioning forward line; flair players were luxuries, distrusted to carry out the team's duties.

Baggio defied these rules. His dribbling ability and skill shone like a beacon; his qualities could not be ignored. He had joined Juventus in a contentious move from Fiorentina having starred for *La Viola*. The deal, done to raise money for stadium renovations, was completed under the cover of darkness to avoid the fans' fury. That Baggio was still able to play was nothing short of a minor miracle. He had shredded his knee ligaments as an 18-year-old at Vicenza with one doctor questioning whether he would ever be able to play again.

The knee operation required 220 internal stitches whilst Baggio sought spiritual calm in his hour of need after discovering he had an allergy to painkillers. Baggio turned to Buddhism, a bold move in a staunchly Roman Catholic country like Italy. The religion's teachings helped him find inner peace and calmness throughout his recovery and, despite a relapse shortly after joining Fiorentina, the man from Caldogno prayed that the bad times were behind him.

With the improvement but ultimate disappointment of Italia 90 in the rear-view mirror, the Italian Football Federation (FIGC) disposed of Vicini's services. In his place came Arrigo Sacchi, whose AC Milan side had captured two European Cups and one Serie A title under his tutelage. Like Baggio, Sacchi's journey to the top had been an arduous one. Never a professional player, Sacchi, like his father, spent time as a shoe salesman before getting the chance to coach at his local club Baracca Lugo. He was 26 years old and spent his formative coaching years watching the great Brazil and Netherlands sides of the 70s. His breakthrough came in 1983 when he was named youth coach at Fiorentina.

Sacchi took over with the *Azzurri* under a cloud having failed to qualify for Euro 92. Immediately he looked to bestow his beliefs and practices on the national team, adopting the same principles that had brought him success at club level. Much to the chagrin of the press, he eliminated the *libero* position and urged his team to control the game by keeping the ball whilst pressing high and hard when they lost it. Defensively, Sacchi put stock in his old Milan back four, favouring a 4-4-2 formation that could convert to a 4-3-3 if required.

To reach these levels of understanding Sacchi attempted to develop a club mentality within the international squad. He faced the wrath of club managers by setting up training camps in which he could go through the minutiae of his tactics as drill after drill was performed until they became second nature. Sacchi's never-ending search for perfection meant there was a revolving door in the national side; throughout two and a half years he called up an astonishing 73 players to his squads.

There was little room in Sacchi's side for individualism, unfortunate when Italy had arguably the world's greatest talent in its ranks. The Baggio conundrum was one Sacchi needed to solve but whilst they were renowned for their defensive brilliance, the *Azzurri* also had a plethora of goalscoring options. The thought of choosing between the aforementioned Baggio, Gianluca Vialli, Pierluigi Casiraghi, Roberto Mancini, Gianfranco Zola, Giuseppe Signori and Daniele Massaro would leave most managers salivating. The manager's high-profile bust-ups with Vialli and Mancini did, however, help Sacchi narrow the decision-making process.

Qualification for USA 94 was secured by a lesser-known member of the squad, Dino Baggio. Unrelated and unfairly called 'the other Baggio', his 83rd-minute strike against Portugal won the three vital points that booked Italy's place on the plane. Preparation in the build-up wasn't ideal, however, especially in a country where you are only one defeat away from the panic button being pressed. Friendly defeats to France and Germany were exacerbated by a 2-1 loss to Serie C2 side Pontedera during another hastily arranged Sacchi training camp. The unlikely yet meaningless loss just two months before the World Cup had the Italian football press calling for the manager's head. The headline of the largest of Italy's daily newspapers, *La Gazzetta dello Sport*, declared, 'Let's send Pontedera to the World Cup'.

The frothing amongst the media did little to dint any confidence within the squad, however. 'The mood was great,' said defender Alessandro Costacurta. 'We [AC Milan] had just become European Champions and we took that confidence into the World Cup,' the *Rossoneri* legend added.

Immediate calls for Sacchi's head were ignored but there were still plenty of question marks surrounding his starting XI when the 22-man squad headed off to the States. There were three goalkeepers, eight defenders, six midfielders and five strikers in the squad. Signori arrived in the USA as Serie A's top goalscorer whilst Zola and Massaro took the places of the excommunicated Vialli and Mancini. The Italian Football Federation (FIGC) had booked all 73 rooms at the Somerset Hills Hotel, surrounded by rolling hills in central New Jersey. The commuter town of Warren was a short hop from the Meadowlands where Italy would play their first game against the Republic of Ireland.

If the knives were still out after the Pontedera debacle, they were being sharpened following a less than auspicious start. Notoriously slow starters in tournaments, Italy were true to form as a Ray Houghton goal gave Ireland an unlikely victory in Group E's opening game. Baggio was quietened by the commanding Paul McGrath and the expected swarm of Italian fans failed to materialise as Giants Stadium was bedecked in the Irish tricolour. Pressure on Sacchi was rising and again the newspapers showed no mercy. The *Gazetta Sportiva* ran with 'What a Sacchi disaster', whilst *La Stampa* called the match a 'legendary fiasco'. Italian restaurateurs bemoaned the performance as their premises emptied at the final whistle, *Corriere dello Sport* matched the sentiment calling it a 'betrayal' and *La Repubblica* failed to give the Irish much credit by saying Sacchi's side was the worst Italy had ever fielded.

The stakes were understandably high five days later when Italy returned to Giants Stadium to face Norway. 'The defeat with Ireland was terrible for morale,' Costacurta remembered. 'The following days there was so much tension coming from outside [the squad] but it had a positive effect on us against Norway.' Sacchi took his customary approach of ringing the changes in his line-up and the Italian press, usually ones to criticise his chopping and changing, were for once in agreement. In defence, the 34-year-old Mauro Tassotti of Milan was dropped for dynamic Parma full-back Antonio Benarrivo whilst a change in shape meant Nicola Berti and Pierluigi Casiraghi replaced Roberto Donadoni and the injured Alberigo Evani. Boos rang out around Giants Stadium during the opening presentations as both Sacchi and Italy's future were on the line.

The opening exchanges saw Italy in the ascendancy. The *Azzurri* pressed and pressured the Norwegians who looked the antithesis of the team that impressed during qualifying. Baggio and Albertini saw shots bend over the bar whilst Dino Baggio brought the best out of Erik Thorstvedt in the Norway goal. With a core of players who made their living playing in England, Egil Olsen's men had more than enough in their arsenal to cause Italy problems, Nottingham Forest pair Alf-Inge Håland and Lars Bohinen both eager to get on the ball and supply the main goal threat, Jostein Flo.

The patience of Norway paid off; Erik Mykland played a clever ball through for Øyvind Leonhardsen who managed to spring the much-vaunted Italian offside trap. Through on goal, the Rosenborg midfielder bore down on Gianluca Pagliuca who, caught in two minds, raced from his goal. Leonhardsen quickly fired a shot across Pagliuca who pushed the effort away with his first touch of the game. However, due to the rush of blood, the Sampdoria custodian had advanced out of the penalty area as his hands made contact with the ball. German referee Helmut Krug was in no doubt: free kick to Norway and a red card for Pagliuca, the first goalkeeper to be sent off in a World Cup.

There were 22 minutes on the clock. Italy were reduced to ten men and heading for the exit door. Luca Marchegiani rose from the bench to take Pagliuca's place between the posts, but which outfield player would make way for the substitute goalkeeper? When the number ten board went up, no one could quite believe it. In a must-win game, Sacchi was sacrificing Roberto Baggio. Seeing his number raised, Baggio stared in disbelief. 'Has he gone mad?' he muttered as Marchegiani took his place.

There was a method to Sacchi's madness, however. A man down in the blistering heat meant a different approach was needed. Sacchi knew his team would need to dig in and every blade of grass would have to be covered if they were to get anything from the game. Baggio had a niggling Achilles tendon issue and Italy couldn't afford any passengers. Although the game had remained goalless, Italy's problems intensified shortly after half-time when captain Franco Baresi stretched to cut out a Leonhardsen pass. The backbone of the Italian defence landed awkwardly and crumpled to the turf, clutching his knee.

Having missed out on qualification for Euro 92, Baresi retired from international football to try to elongate his club career. His heir apparent, Sampdoria's Marco Lanna, had a debut to forget in the first World Cup qualifier with Switzerland, leaving Sacchi to persuade his former player to re-join the *Azzurri* fold. The 34-year-old had been part of the squad that won at España 82 but had his path to the first team blocked by the late great Gaetano Scirea so the title of 'World Cup winner' seemed a hollow one. Baresi was back in time for the second qualification game, contributing to a clean sheet in a 0-0 draw with Scotland. The rugged centre-half also took back the captain's armband from Vialli, who within a month was cast into the international wilderness by Sacchi.

Back at Giants Stadium, Baresi couldn't continue and Parma's Luigi Apolloni was called upon to replace him, winning only his second Italy cap. With their first-choice goalkeeper, captain and star attacker absent, the *Azzurri* faced a make-or-break final 40 minutes if they were to save their World Cup. Norway mixed up their play as they bombarded the Italian defence with a combination of direct balls and short, sharp passes. The trap Norway fell into was one of their own making, however. After their 1-0 win over Mexico in the opening game, a point against Italy would all but secure their passage to the knockout stages.

The Italians persevered; having sacrificed Baggio, Sacchi pushed Signori out wide, leaving Casiraghi as the lone striker. Their defiance paid off with Håland booked for a foul on Italy's makeshift left-winger near the touchline. The Lazio man dusted himself off to send a free kick curling into the penalty area where Dino Baggio manoeuvred between two defenders to head home from eight yards.

Norway were unable to shift gears whilst the patched-up Italians resembled the walking wounded. A challenge from Jostein Flo on Paolo Maldini left the AC Milan defender with a bandaged left foot, reducing the *Azzurri* to nine men whilst running repairs were administered. Dino Baggio was doubled over with cramp and was visibly limping as Krug finally blew for full time. Against the odds, Italy had won and were still very much alive in the World Cup. Sacchi explained his decision to replace Baggio after Pagliuca's sending off: 'I did it for him and for the sake of the team,' he said. 'I needed nine players who could run a lot, he can be decisive against Mexico.' It was a gamble that could have cost him his job but Sacchi, resplendent in his garish green training attire, lived to fight another day.

Whilst Italy's World Cup endeavour appeared to be back on track, the fitness of their captain was a concern. The night after the Norway game, Baresi found he couldn't straighten his leg. He was rushed to the Lennox Hill hospital in Manhattan where a scan was undertaken to try to discover the extent of the knee injury. The good news was no ligament damage was found, but the Italian captain had suffered a longitudinal fracture to his medial meniscus. Arthroscopic surgery was required and quickly. The Milan club doctor cut short a holiday in St Moritz and headed straight to Manhattan.

On the evening of 24 June, one day after the Norway game, orthopaedic specialist Dr Elliott B. Hershman performed the 20-minute procedure on Baresi. The defender had the same operation on his left knee back in 1985 where the recovery took two and a half months but now, at his age, it could easily spell the end of his career. Having missed the recent European Cup Final through suspension, Baresi was determined that, should Italy get to the World Cup Final in 24 days, he would be ready. The captain also wanted to stay with the squad, so the morning after the operation he returned to Somerset Hills where his wife Maura and son Edoardo joined him. The clock was ticking and within two days Baresi was walking freely. Performances so far suggested Italy's chances of making the World Cup Final were slim, but for their captain, the fitness race was on.

The World Cup 'Group of Death' couldn't have been more evenly poised. All four teams had played two games, winning one and losing the other. Italy would need a positive result over Mexico in the final group game if they were to avoid the ignominy of being the first Italian national team in 20 years not to make the latter stages of the competition. It was a task made all the more difficult with the absence of both Pagliuca and Baresi.

During the first 13 World Cups, Mexico had only advanced from the group stages at tournaments they had hosted. At USA 94 they had as good a chance as any. The group couldn't have been any more evenly poised going into the final round of games and *El Tri* would be backed by a partisan crowd of 53,000 at Washington DC's RFK Stadium.

Chances were few and far between in the first half with neither team willing to risk conceding. Baggio again was quiet, with Mexican captain Ignacio Ambríz paying him particularly close attention. Sacchi kept Serie A dangerman Signori on the left flank and chose to replace the ineffective Casiraghi at half-time. On in his place came Massaro, whose impact was almost immediate. Albertini lofted an exquisite chipped pass from the centre circle that the Milan striker controlled on his chest before firing underneath the neon pink jersey of Jorge Campos in the Mexico goal. With the score in the other game going Italy's way, they were now top of Group E and looked to have put their topsy-turvy beginning to the tournament behind them.

Signori continued to provide a threat in his new-found position. His pass played in Dino Baggio, who was felled under a challenge in the penalty area. Despite several protestations, Argentinian referee Francisco Lamolina was unmoved. It was a decision that threatened to haunt the *Azzurri* as Mexico levelled shortly after. Italy's usually strict defence failed to clear its lines; Mexico striker Carlos Hermosillo laid the ball off to Marcelino Bernal some 25 yards from goal. Bernal avoided a Signori sliding tackle before firing a low shot from the edge of the area through Maldini's legs and past the despairing dive of Marchegiani. Mexico were level and with their third goal in the tournament had gone from fourth to first in Group E.

Massaro, Signori and Berti had further chances but Campos saved everything that came his way. With Baggio again a non-factor, both sides had to settle for a draw. Mexico had put in a professional performance, showing a resolute defence whilst taking advantage of a rare Italian defensive lapse. Norway and the Republic of Ireland ended goalless in the group's other game, so all four teams ended on the same points. Thanks to Bernal's effort, Mexico finished top on goals scored whilst Ireland's shock win over the *Azzurri* confirmed them as Group E runners-up. Italy would have to wait and see if they would qualify as one of the four best third-placed teams. Russia's hammering of Cameroon confirmed it and the *Azzurri* scraped through to the knockout rounds where a buoyant Nigeria awaited.

Progress through the group stages had done little to lift the pressure off Sacchi and the players back home, with Juventus owner Gianni Agnelli likening his record signing Baggio's performance against Mexico to that of a wet rabbit. Heading into the knockout stages, the stakes were raised; it was now win or go home. Cometh the hour, cometh the man.

As in the Norway game, when the chips were down, Italy found a way. A goal down and reduced to ten men, the *Azzurri* were yet again staring a World Cup exit in the face. Nigeria had failed to reach the attacking heights of their group games but looked to have done enough to expand their reputation as one of world football's emerging forces. Paolo Maldini had an afternoon to forget, firstly ricocheting the ball into Emmanuel Amunike's path for the Super Eagles' goal and then extremely lucky to stay on the pitch after desperately hauling Rashidi Yekini to the ground.

It was twelve years to the day since Italy beat West Germany in the World Cup final, the heroics of Paolo Rossi and Marco Tardelli forever etched in Italian football folklore. With 105 seconds of the 90 minutes remaining, Baggio's World Cup finally ignited as he brought Italy level. Defender Roberto Mussi dribbled his way into the right-hand side of the penalty area, and perhaps realising the enormity of the situation he played a pass into Baggio's path. Quick as a flash, *Il Divin Codino* had his very own 'Rossi moment' as he swept the ball into the far corner of the net, out of the reach of Peter Rufai in goal.

As the game went into extra time Italy's confidence grew whilst Nigeria's usual swagger withered away. Baggio took control, and picking up the ball on the corner of the penalty area he scooped a high pass for Benarrivo to run on to. Defender Agustin Eguavoen had allowed the Parma man goal-side of him and inexplicably body-checked the defender to the ground.

Mexican referee Arturo Brizio Carter, who had also controversially sent Zola off in the 76th minute, ran to the penalty spot, whistle in mouth and pointed towards the goal. Penalty to Italy, and who else to take it but Baggio, who sent Rufai the wrong way as the ball kissed the post on its way in. Italy led in extra time but there was still time for one more Nigeria chance, the unsung Dino Baggio this time coming to the *Azzurri*'s rescue by clearing a Yekini effort off the line.

Suddenly there had been a shift in expectations. Italy had made it through to the quarter-finals and if *Il Divin Codino* had woken from his slumber, who knew how far they could go. Baggio later stated that he felt all nervousness and anxiety leave his body when he scored against Nigeria and that defeat was not an option. 'Baggio had played poorly to this point,' said Costacurta, who would go on to win 59 caps for the *Azzurri*. 'Until his 89th minute goal against Nigeria, then from that moment he became the strongest in the world.'

Despite the heroic comeback Sacchi again faced criticism, this time due to the impending recall of Pagliuca to the side after serving his suspension. Rumours emerged that Baggio could be a doubt as cramp had ravaged his muscles in extra time. However, nothing would keep him from facing their Iberian neighbours Spain, who in turn had enjoyed three days' more rest than the Italians.

The World Cup had been fairly non-descript for *La Roja* up to this point; draws with South Korea and Germany were followed up with a routine win over Bolivia in Group C's final game. A comfortable 3-0 victory against Roy Hodgson's Switzerland in Washington DC set up the tie with Italy in the humid mist of Foxboro Stadium. Sacchi's men had resorted to taking vitamins and salts to aid their recovery with several players snakebitten with cramps during each game.

Sacchi made three more changes alongside recalling Pagliuca. Another formation shift saw Signori drop to the bench, replaced by Antonio Conte, whilst Mauro Tassotti was preferred in defence and Nicola Berti swapped places with Dino Baggio on the subs bench. Despite much talk of their walking wounded, Italy shot out of the blocks, much to the surprise of Javier Clemente's side. The *Azzurri* went ahead after 25 minutes: following patient hold-up play by Roberto Donadoni, the recalled Baggio measured a beautiful 30-yard strike that swerved away from Spanish goalkeeper Andoni Zubizarreta's outstretched arms and into the net.

Both sides traded chances in the remainder of the first half and *Il Divin Codino* pulled two efforts wide of the goal as the *Azzurri* went into the second half with the lead. As the hour mark approached, Spain's patience and persistence paid off. The pace of the game had quickened significantly and it was *La Roja* who benefitted when they broke down their left side. A Sergi cut-back was sidestepped by Otero before José Caminero's shot glanced off the foot of Benarrivo and over Pagliuca to level proceedings.

Sacchi had already thrown Berti and Signori into the fray but still the *Azzurri* failed to gain control of the game. Extra time beckoned and Italy found themselves hemmed into their own half; substitute Julio Salinas almost won it for Spain, but his weak effort only found Pagliuca's legs. Italy had been reduced to playing on the counter-attack, something of an alien concept for a Sacchi side, but when the ball arrived at Benarrivo's feet there was only one thing on his mind.

Glancing up, the Parma full-back found Berti who in turn played the ball on to Signori. With a challenge imminent the substitute strained every sinew to knock the ball on once more, this time towards Roberto Baggio who was now in a one-on-one with Zubizarreta. The experienced Barcelona glovesman advanced from his goal, narrowing the angle and forcing Baggio into a decision. With a drop of the shoulder, Baggio toed the ball around the keeper and away from the goal. A second touch took him even wider, but he wrapped his boot around the Questra ball and shot through the despairing slide of Spain defender Abelardo on the goal line. He barely had the energy to celebrate, just blowing a kiss to the adoring *tifosi* in the stands above.

There was still time for more drama as Jon Andoni Goikoetxea fired a cross into the Italian penalty area. As the ball sailed out for a throw-in, Spanish attacker Luis Enrique lay prone in the penalty area. Hungarian referee Sándor Puhl remained nonplussed, but as a groggy and angry Enrique got to his feet, blood was seen gushing from a facial wound. The furious Spaniard had to be restrained as he fired expletives towards the accused perpetrator Tassotti, who protested his innocence to the quizzical Spanish players. Replays showed Tassotti, out of the view of Puhl, had levelled Enrique with a vicious elbow that appeared to have broken his nose. In these pre-VAR days play continued and both Tassotti and Italy had escaped immediate repercussions.

Puhl blew for full time and many of the exhausted players sank to their knees. Sacchi blew out his cheeks in relief as inexplicably the *Azzurri* were now one game away from what seemed an unlikely World Cup Final. Baggio placed his hands on his knees and whispered a prayer whilst a banner saying, *'Vola, Roby Baggio, Vola'* ('Fly, Roby Baggio, Fly') hung above him. As World Cup surprise package Bulgaria awaited back in New Jersey, it appeared that Baggio had found his wings just at the precise time.

Whilst Clemente was magnanimous in defeat, Spain were apoplectic at the brutality dished out by Tassotti in the game's closing stages. FIFA's disciplinary panel viewed the videotape the following day and handed down an unprecedented eight-game ban for 'intentional serious violent conduct', accompanied by a $16,000 fine. Gianfranco Zola would miss the semi-final too as he served the second of his two-match ban for the red card against Nigeria, but Tassotti would potentially have to wait until the seventh game of the Euro 96 qualifiers before he could don the famous blue shirt again.

The Italian American support was now out in full force as the *Azzurri* looked to put the ghosts of their ponderous early performances at Giants Stadium to bed. The Roberto Baggio of the Ireland defeat had been replaced by the player the world had been yearning to see. His confidence had spread like wildfire throughout the squad and, just as they did against Spain, the *Azzurri* flew out of the traps in the semi-final.

Bulgaria looked to stifle Baggio, with Zlatko Yankov given the unenviable task of man-marking him. Sacchi ordered his side to press the Bulgarians, noting them to be at their most dangerous when allowed time on the ball. On 20 minutes, the *Azzurri* won a throw-in on the left. Donadoni quickly threw the ball to Baggio who was shadowed as ever by Yankov. In one movement, *Il Divin Codino* controlled the throw, turned inside his marker and headed for goal. Before Petar Hubchev could judge the impending situation, Baggio had skipped around him and bent an exquisite shot around fellow defender Trifon Ivanov and under goalkeeper Boris Mikhailov.

From an innocuous throw-in to 1-0 in the blink of an eye, Baggio had saved his best performance for Bulgaria. Moments later he set up Albertini whose drive cannoned off Mikhailov's post as Bulgaria desperately scrambled to stay in the game. Albertini then turned provider and, in a moment akin to his assist for Massaro's goal in the Mexico game, deftly chipped a pass over the top of the Bulgarian defence. One step ahead of the opposition, Baggio raced through the right channel, timing his run to perfection. He allowed the ball to bounce once before hitting a low shot past Mikhailov into the far corner. It was 2-0 with 25 minutes gone and it suddenly seemed a long way back for Bulgaria.

Unperturbed, Bulgaria fought their way back into the game and two minutes before half-time they were awarded a penalty. Alessandro Costacurta clumsily fouled Nasko Sirakov as he closed in on the Italy goal. Hristo Stoichkov sent Pagliuca the wrong way and in turn scored his sixth goal of the tournament. The penalty gave Bulgaria belief and the Italian defence had to be at their resolute best to keep them at bay for the remainder of the second half. Midfielders Krasimir Balakov and Yordan Letchkov both had chances to level proceedings and when Baggio was substituted clutching his hamstring with 20 minutes remaining, Italy looked to be hanging on.

Signori was brought on in Baggio's place, an able replacement who again answered the call from his manager when needed. Baggio looked close to tears in the dugout as he stood with his arm around Italian legend Gigi Riva's shoulders. His awakening had taken Italy to within touching distance of the World Cup Final, but it looked as though the travails of the last three weeks had finally taken their toll.

As French referee Joël Quiniou blew the full-time whistle, Baggio's emotions took over. He sobbed in the arms of namesake Dino and other team-mates as the enormity of the situation hit home. Time would tell the extent of Baggio's hamstring issue but for now, against the odds Italy were headed to Pasadena for the final. 'This is my life,' Baggio explained to reporters post-match. 'It's made of sweat and tears, but I cried because I was very, very happy.' He had scored five of Italy's last six goals but now joined his captain Baresi in a race against time to be fit for the biggest game of their lives.

Chapter Fifteen

The Ugly Duckling

HEADING INTO the summer of 1994, Brazil faced a conundrum. It had been 24 years since their triumph in Mexico where they dazzled and thrilled, culminating in full-back Carlos Alberto's thunderous drive at the Azteca Stadium that secured their third World Cup. What should have been their crowning glory instead saw *O Seleção* suffer something of an identity crisis.

They huffed and puffed their way throughout the remainder of the decade as they failed to match the rhythm and grace of the 1970 side. The Brazil of 1982 was a throwback to the rip-roaring teams of old but they were brought crashing back to earth by the nous and guile of an Italian side drilled to the nth degree. With the joy of the 1970 World Cup victory long worn off, the Brazilian Football Confederation (CBF) responded by building a new training complex at Granja Comary in Rio in an attempt to rediscover the magic ahead of Mexico 86. However, this didn't yield the expected results with Sebastião Lazaroni's side producing Brazil's worst World Cup finish since 1966.

The man tasked with leading Brazil back to the promised land had a winning pedigree. Carlos Alberto Parreira was part of the physio team at Mexico 70 where he worked alongside coach Mário Zagallo and had spent the majority of the last two decades managing in the Middle East. Despite being a less than glamorous appointment, desperate times were upon Brazil. Whatever Parreira's formula would be, it had to be a winning one. Parreira sensed the size of the job at hand and turned to Zagallo, persuading the two-time World Cup winner to return to the national team set-up as an advisor.

Heading into the 1994 World Cup, Brazilian sport was at its lowest ebb and faith had been lost in *O Seleção*. A poll conducted in Brazil suggested a mere ten per cent of the general public believed they could recapture their crown in the USA. When the legendary São Paulo-born racing driver Ayrton Senna was killed in a Formula One crash a month before the World Cup began, a mourning nation looked to the football team for solace.

Parreira was a pragmatic technocrat, a student of the organised and methodical approach that European sides displayed. Approaching the tournament, however, he retained two very important parts of Brazilian football's DNA: attacking full-backs and a 4-4-2 formation. Brazil would play their first two Group B games in Stanford, California, before ending the group stage indoors at the Pontiac Silverdome in Detroit. Parreira realised the suffocating temperatures would be as important a factor as the opposition and planned accordingly. There would have to be sacrifices.

Brazil's plan was to own the middle of the pitch, control possession and dictate the tempo of games. Goals would come from Romário and Bebeto, of this Parreira was sure. There would be two players feeding the ball to them whilst, behind, Dunga and Mauro Silva would provide the solidity missing from previous tournaments. The former had spent the last seven years in Europe, primarily in Italy before joining Germany's Stuttgart in 1993. He was part of the silver medal-winning squad at the Los Angeles Olympics in 1984 then the triumphant Copa América side five years later. The 4-4-2 would resemble more of a 4-2-2-2 in practice; the width would be provided by the full-backs Jorginho and Leonardo, with two players sat between the back four and the attacking midfielders.

It was hoped that the two main beneficiaries of this added defensive shield would be the attacking pair of Romário and Bebeto, a footballing equivalent of chalk and cheese, a brash cockiness partnered with a calm modesty. The Diabolical Duo's backgrounds were at opposite ends of the scale. Bebeto was the fifth of eight children and enjoyed a moderately comfortable middle-class upbringing. Romário grew up in Jacarezinho, one of Rio's largest *favelas*. 'Romário was always late for training while Bebeto was the punctual, exemplary athlete,' recalled Brazilian journalist Marluci Martins. 'Bebeto is the good boy, married for many years to the mother of his children whilst Romário had the bad boy lifestyle, with a reputation for sneaking women into training camps. The ball was the secret of this union [between Bebeto and Romário].'

The two strikers were the perfect foil for each other. Romário's stocky, low centre of gravity meaning he was difficult to shake off the ball combined with a deadly eye for goal. Bebeto was lither, as capable of dropping back to get on the ball as he was in the six-yard box. Both were also gifted with an exquisite touch and had moved to Europe before the finals. Romário joined his strike partner in Spain 12 months before the finals, signing for Barcelona having scored an imperious 165 goals in 167 appearances for PSV Eindhoven in the Netherlands' Eredivisie.

Since starting out with Vasco da Gama, Romário hadn't stopped scoring, boosting his value as much as his ego. Bebeto, on the other hand, received his first call-up to *O Seleção* whilst at Flamengo in 1985 but found goals hard to come by with some critics wondering whether he would struggle to live up to the pressures of wearing the hallowed shirt. The Seoul Olympics in 1988 saw the debut of the Diabolical Duo. Romário top-scored with seven as the young Brazilians made the final, losing 2-1 to the Soviet Union after extra time in front of 74,000 fans.

There was no disputing Romário's goalscoring record yet previous concerns over his attitude and ego were never far away. Brazil-based football journalist Tim Vickery felt that Parreira had learnt from previous conflicts and was adamant it wouldn't happen again. 'Romário roomed with Dunga throughout the tournament, all they needed was for him to rein in his behaviour for four weeks.' Parreira and Zagallo knew how pivotal an in-form Romário would be if Brazil were to win their fourth title. 'Getting him on board was key,' added Vickery.

Martins, who covered the tournament for Rio daily newspaper *O Dia*, was well placed to see how important Romário was, not only to *O Seleção* but also to the people of Brazil. 'We're football fanatics, the call-up of Romário brought optimism. He was a portrait of the Brazilian people, due to his rise and his poor origins,' Martins recalled. However, Romário's place in the squad was far from guaranteed. 'The relationship [between Romário and Parreira] was bad but there was professionalism.'

When striker Müller broke down in training the clamour for Romário's inclusion gained momentum. 'Muller confided in me at the end of the training session that he felt something in his leg but asked for it not to be published until the following morning,' Martins recalled. 'At that moment I knew that if Muller was cut Parreira would recall Romário and that is what happened. When Romário was called up and when his goals secured World Cup qualification he was stamping his passport to the USA.'

Ahead of their opening two games in California's Bay Area, Brazil trained at Santa Clara University whilst setting up base in the nearby town of Los Gatos. The town's inhabitants took the squad to their hearts. Over $25,000 was raised to ensure the players' safety for the duration of their time there and a local statue was adorned in the colours of the Brazilian flag. The love was reciprocated. Local youngsters were invited for a once-in-a-lifetime opportunity to train with the squad as their parents were tempted to try salsa lessons. The town of 30,000 inhabitants offered Brazil a secluded resort for the duration of their stay in the beautiful Villa Felice, which impressed Parreira no end.

As the Brazilians settled into their surroundings receiving the red-carpet treatment from town mayor Roger Attaway, there was the little matter of a World Cup starting 2,000 miles away in Chicago. Brazil's tournament kicked off against Russia in Group B; Cameroon faced Sweden in the other fixture. With Parreira hoping the Romário issue had been solved, his next concern was a patched-up defence, an area that had suffered significant upheaval over the previous 12 months. Firstly, the uncompromising and experienced Júlio César clashed with the CBF and was out of the squad before two injuries plunged the back four into disarray.

Two starting centre-halves from the previous World Cup, Ricardo Gomes and Carlos Mozer, both fell foul of the injury bug. Benfica's Mozer pulled out with a liver condition whilst Gomes tore a calf muscle at the 11th hour, leaving Parreira to not only re-tool the defence but also find a new leader, with Gomes set to captain the side for the second consecutive World Cup. Missing three first-choice centre-halves would have crippled most teams yet even after these injuries, having the likes of Roma's Aldair still able to make the starting XI proved the defensive strength in depth, a refreshing change given their reputation for producing attackers.

A crowd of just over 81,000 braved the searing midday sun. Ricardo Rocha replaced Gomes in the heart of the defence with Raí of Paris Saint-Germain seemingly overcoming his injury problems to take over the captain's armband. In a sign of the direction in which the Brazilian game was heading, a mere two home-based players were named in O Seleção's starting XI: Rocha and Zinho.

The Russians made their first tournament appearance since the break-up of the Soviet Union, having played their debut international match a mere 22 months earlier. Embattled coach Pavel Sadyrin fielded an experienced side, predominantly made up of players from Spartak Moscow.

Brazil were resounding favourites and began the game in such fashion, dominating the early exchanges. Skill and tenacity from Jorginho resulted in a back-post cross that Bebeto acrobatically blazed over the bar. The Deportivo de La Coruña man mouthed a silent prayer; the perfect start had passed him and Brazil by. A pre-tournament decision not to replace the Stanford Stadium pitch looked to be a churlish one as the ball bobbled and jerked around. Brazil, however, adjusted accordingly, looking to make short, incisive passes on the inconsistent surface.

On 25 minutes, Bebeto shrugged off the early disappointment of his miss to play a major role in the opening goal. Leonardo's pace forced a corner which Bebeto took, swinging the ball in towards the edge of the six-yard box. Romário, quick as a flash, shrugged off his marker to steer the ball on the volley inside the unmarked back post and give his side the lead. The striker whose goals rubber-stamped Brazil's qualification was off the mark as the team swamped each other in celebration. It was something that seemed impossible in the not too distant past when the enigmatic frontman refused to sit with team-mates and tested the patience of players and coaches alike.

A goal inside the first half-hour was perfect for Brazil as the sun beat down on Palo Alto and energy levels deteriorated dramatically as the game wore on. Already Jorginho and Leonardo had enjoyed numerous forays down the flanks as Parreira's plan seemed to be paying dividends. Russia attempted to break the Brazilian's control of the game, yet they couldn't get close enough to the canary-yellow shirts with a quick pass always on offer. Zinho fired a left-footed attempt at the Russian goal, which Dmitri Kharine gathered at the second attempt as the first half drew to a close.

Horns and drums reverberated around the sold-out stadium with the open-aired stands and running track doing nothing to detract from the atmosphere. Whilst Russia had defaulted into a defensive shape during the majority of the first half, the opening chance of the second period fell to defender Sergei Gorlukovich whose shot bounced wide as Taffarel scrambled across his goal.

Despite Russia showing more gumption in the opening period of the second half, Brazil put the game out of reach on 53 minutes. Romário was again instrumental in the goal, receiving the ball into feet with his back to goal. He swiftly turned his marker before slotting the ball through another defender's legs and bursting into the penalty area. A desperate Vladislav Ternavsky was left with little option but to scythe the Brazilian striker down leaving Mauritian referee Lee Kim Chong no option but to point to the spot.

Captain Raí stepped up and converted the spot kick that confirmed Brazil's routine opening win. The goal meant Raí had achieved the same feat as his elder brother Sócrates, who 12 years earlier also scored on his World Cup debut, his coincidentally coming against the Soviet Union. Brazil may have been far from their devastating best but, following a 2-2 draw in the other group game between Sweden and Cameroon the day before, *O Seleção* were top of Group B. However, the injury bug bit again with Brazil losing their fourth centre-half. This time Gomes's replacement Ricardo Rocha limped off after 75 minutes.

The Central Africans were up next with over 83,000 fans watching on as Brazil looked to all but secure their passage to the next round. Aldair replaced the injured Rocha in defence; Ronaldão was allowed to be called up late and travelled from Japan, where he played his club football, to take his place on the bench. He gained the 'ã' in his name to differentiate between himself and a 17-year-old striker who was in the squad and went by the same name.

Any worries over Brazil's supposed lack of midfield creativity was almost rendered obsolete due to the guile and pace of Bebeto and Romário. Football was reduced to its simplest of forms; well-timed balls put into danger areas provided Brazil with all they needed, the Diabolical Duo would do the rest. This was no truer in the build-up to Brazil's first goal. Dunga dispossessed Louis-Paul M'Fédé in midfield before playing an exquisite outside-of-the-foot pass to Romário. The man known as *O Baixinho* ('the Short One') took the ball in his stride with one touch, then set off on a foot race with three Cameroonian defenders. With impeccable timing, he left his pursuers in his wake and toed the ball under the advancing Joseph-Antoine Bell in the Cameroon goal to put his side ahead six minutes before half-time.

The second half began with Brazil looking to again control possession and with it the game's tempo. Cameroon, however, could feel aggrieved not to have been awarded a penalty when a rash challenge on David Embé from Márcio Santos went unpunished, a feeling exacerbated when defender Rigobert Song saw red on 63 minutes. Bebeto looked to break down the right wing and Song lunged in, wiping out the slight Brazilian with no hint of reaching the ball. Mexican referee Arturo Brizio Carter was in little doubt and raised the red card leaving the Indomitable Lions down to ten men.

Just two minutes later further salt was rubbed into the wound when, following nice play down the right side, Jorginho received a no-look pass from Dunga before curling a cross on to the head of Márcio Santos who planted the ball past a flailing Bell to make it 2-0. Brazil were dominant, taking advantage of their numerical supremacy as Romário dragged a shot wide before Bell saved well from Bebeto after a well-worked free kick. On 72 minutes the dagger blow came when Romário shook off Hans Agbo but could not work the ball under Bell this time. The Saint-Étienne glovesman ushered the ball away from goal but only into the path of Bebeto who slotted in from the tightest of angles. The Brazilians again celebrated as a squad with many players running to the sideline to embrace others. Two games, two wins and a united *O Seleção* were on their way to the knockout stages.

Sweden too had scored three goals in their game with Russia to keep in touch with Brazil, knowing that a win in the final game at the Silverdome would take them through as group winners. This game gave the first warning signs of Brazil's fallibility as the step-up in quality of the opposition seemingly took them by surprise. A goal from Lille's Kennet Andersson gave the Swedes a well-deserved lead, the towering striker controlling a pass then lobbing Cláudio Taffarel before Mauro Silva could make a challenge. Brazil were rocked. It was the first goal they had conceded in the tournament and a clear message that not only could they be breached, they could also be beaten.

Moments later the lead could have been extended further when Tomas Brolin, instrumental in the first goal, saw his cross blocked by Leonardo as striker Henrik Larsson waited to pounce. The half-time whistle couldn't have come at a worse moment for Sweden, who were still very much in the ascendancy. Whatever Parreira said at the break worked as, within 90 seconds of the restart, Brazil were level. Romário advanced unimpeded and toe-poked a low bobbling shot past Thomas Ravelli in the Sweden goal for the equaliser and his third in as many games. Brazil now sensed blood and Sweden were hanging on for their lives.

Brazil couldn't find a second goal though and the game petered out into a draw, giving both sides a pass through to the knockout stages of the competition. Brazil's 100 per cent record had gone and whilst progress in the tournament had been secured, a huge improvement was required from the ever-demanding press back home.

Rio's daily newspaper *O Globo* ran with a deafening headline declaring a 'Show of Incompetence' whilst the *Jornal do Brasil* stated the national team 'played poorly and were booed' under a headline of 'Wake Up, Parreira'. Inside they slammed the coach and two of his creative outlets in captain Raí and attacking midfield partner Zinho. Parreira was defiant, however, saying that changes would not be made in his midfield as Brazil looked ahead to a return to Palo Alto and a meeting with the hosts in the last 16.

The difference in the two sides was evident. Brazil had won three World Cups, the USA had only won three games in their finals history. On paper, the result should never have been in doubt, but the Sweden game had perhaps unconsciously planted a seed of doubt in Brazilian minds. They were imperfect and as each game brought the final that one step closer, the pressure was beginning to mount on Parreira and his squad.

Football is a religion to the people of Brazil and with it comes understandable pressure. It is said that *O Seleção* has 150 million coaches. Parreira had to remain steadfast to his beliefs; it was too late to change the squad and his tactics now. If they were to secure their fourth title, they would be doing it his way and his way alone. This was despite line-up suggestions from Brazilian president Itamar Franco, Pelé's request for six changes and Parreira's own mother telling her son to pick the young phenomenon Ronaldo.

There was one change from the Sweden game as captain Raí made way for Mazinho, the busy Palmeiras midfielder. 'Parreira knew there was a chance he would have to drop Raí at some point,' explained Vickery. 'Even before the tournament started, he simply hadn't played enough games for his club.' The Paris Saint-Germain midfielder's already diminished fitness levels had taken a battering in the soaring temperatures. Parreira's reasoning behind this decision divulged to Vickery years later was simple: 'It was better to have an injured player than a tired one.'

There was no room for passengers, not now one false step could mean the end of the tournament. Jorginho was favourite to receive the captain's armband but Parreira turned to his loyal lieutenant, Dunga, the man who, despite the press's reservations about his abilities, was key to delivering Parreira's game plan.

Cameroon's 42-year-old Roger Milla becomes the World Cup's oldest goalscorer (again) whilst Oleg Salenko bags five goals in one game.

Diego Maradona talks to the media during a brief press conference following his expulsion.

In what's widely regarded as the game of the tournament, unfancied Romania led by captain Gheorghe Hagi face Argentina.

Sweden advance to the quarter-finals of a World Cup for the first time since they were hosts in 1958.

Hopeful fans gather in the Palo Alto sun on America's Independence Day to see the home nation face Brazil.

Bebeto breaches the hosts' defence and breaks the hearts of 80,000 home fans to book his side a place in the last eight.

Brazil's Branco smashes home a free kick against the Netherlands.

Yordan Letchkov completes the shock turnaround for Bulgaria in the quarter-final win over Germany.

Kennet Andersson sends the game with Romania to a penalty shoot-out after an extra-time equaliser for the ten men of Sweden.

Shocked fans make their feelings known after news of Andrés Escobar's murder reaches American shores.

The Rose Bowl in Pasadena. Opening in 1922, it played host to eight matches during USA 94 including the final in front of 94,194 fans.

The talismanic Hristo Stoichkov's six goals propel Bulgaria to an unlikely fourth place finish.

Italy's Paolo Maldini and Brazil's Romario face off for their countries having met two months earlier in the Champions League Final where AC Milan beat Barcelona 4-0.

After 120 energy-sapping scoreless minutes, the 1994 final is the first World Cup to be decided by penalty shoot-out.

Roberto Baggio and Franco Baresi console each other after penalty heartbreak for the Azzurri.

Captain Dunga lifts Brazil's fourth World Cup.

Brazil manager Carlos Alberto Parreira is hoisted aloft by his players after ending a 24-year trophy drought.

Under such scrutiny, it is a testament to Parreira that he remained stoic and didn't falter. 'Being the coach of Brazil is like sitting in a coconut shy,' said Vickery. 'When you win it's down to the players; when you lose all fingers point to the coach.' Brazil had been nowhere near the attacking fluidity of previous incarnations throughout the group stages yet they remained three games away from a final that, should they reach it, would be Parreira's final game in charge. An escape from the goldfish bowl and a return to club football was his likely destination.

For all that the USA had achieved in qualifying from the group stages, they offered little in an attacking sense against Brazil. They harried and chased their opponents with defenders Marcelo Balboa and Alexi Lalas in solid form at the back. Coach Bora Milutinović had craved more possession from his midfield and when Leonardo was red-carded for a brutal elbow on Tab Ramos shortly before half-time, they had a numerical advantage too. Parreira didn't withdraw either of his front two, realising they were his best hope of scoring that elusive goal.

This proved to be the case and it was Bebeto this time who struck the single, crucial goal on 73 minutes. A penetrating run from Romário pulled defenders out of position and he slid the ball to his strike partner whose shot evaded a sliding Lalas and goalkeeper Tony Meola before finding the far corner. The ten men of Brazil had overcome the hosts, much to the relief of Parreira and his 150 million critics back home. Brazil were far from convincing again, their over-reliance on the Diabolical Duo becoming more and more evident with each game. Brazil's hopes of success hinged on their continued goalscoring as the Netherlands awaited in the last eight. A further change was needed in the Brazilian defence with the suspended Leonardo replaced by the veteran of three World Cups, Branco. The press had a field day. The 30-year-old would be up against the flying Dutch winger Marc Overmars having not played a game in over a month. The left-back position was pinpointed as Brazil's Achilles heel; the offensive element that Leonardo brought to the position would be gone and with it a major part of Brazil's attacking intensity.

The Dutch were enjoying their second consecutive World Cup following a barren period in the 1980s after two runners-up places in the 1974 and 78 tournaments. They had progressed as winners of their group despite a defeat to neighbours Belgium in Orlando and swatted the Republic of Ireland aside in the last 16. They had improved on their placing at Italia 90 and appeared more than capable of making life difficult for Brazil as they squared off at the Cotton Bowl in Dallas.

Other than the enforced change at left-back, Parreira put out the same side that squeaked past the USA in the previous round. Unusually, both sides lined up sporting their change kits; Brazil in blue and their Dutch opponents in white. A cagey first half saw neither side able to break the deadlock, showing no sign of the drama that was due to unfold during the second half.

The game burst into life on 52 minutes when a raking ball forward by Aldair found Bebeto wide on the left-hand side. The *Dépor* man often drifted on to the periphery of the attack, making himself available to team-mates time and again. Upon taking control of the ball, Romário began his run and a pinpoint pass across the defenders was met on the bounce by *O Baixinho* who prodded it past a bewildered Ed de Goey. It was Romário's fourth goal and he slumped to his knees and raised his arms in celebration.

Both strikers again had their parts to play ten minutes later when Brazil doubled their lead. A huge kick was launched by de Goey but Branco strode forward and met the descending ball with his head. The Dutch defence was static, awaiting the linesman's flag to be raised as Romário strolled back onside. The flag never came and Bebeto was the first to react as he ran between the defence, skipped past a last-ditch challenge from Jan Wouters then eloquently rounded de Goey and stroked home. A gleeful Bebeto wheeled away in celebration, swinging his arms in a sideways motion, a gesture to his expectant wife Denise who was back in Brazil. Romário and Mazinho joined him as the three Brazilians rocked their arms in unison, providing one of the tournament's lasting images. The Dutch were furious but the goal stood and two goals in ten minutes appeared to have all but sealed Brazil's place in the semi-finals.

The Dutch had other ideas and the *Oranje* struck back almost immediately. A long throw-in by Rob Witschge fell to Dennis Bergkamp inside the Brazil penalty area. With three defenders bearing down on him, he enjoyed a lucky ricochet which brought the ball back into his path before placing a side-footed effort past Taffarel. The Inter Milan striker had the bit between his teeth now and almost brought his side level on 75 minutes, when a quick one-two left him in space before his cross was blocked by Santos. The men in white appealed for handball yet Costa Rican referee Rodrigo Badilla shook his head and merely signalled for a corner kick.

Overmars, who had been adequately shackled by Branco, whipped a right-footed ball into the penalty area where Aron Winter, one of the shortest men on the pitch, headed past a hesitant Taffarel and into the net. The game was level and the Netherlands were in the ascendancy as the clock ticked down to the final ten minutes. Branco had stuck to his task masterfully and on 81 minutes received the ball with space to run into. Shrugging off previous doubts over his fitness, the reserve left-back surged infield with Dutch defenders scrambling back into position. He appeared to be clipped from behind and shunted into a covering defender. Both sides appealed for a free kick as Branco writhed around on the floor clutching his ribs somewhat dramatically. Feeling that Branco's momentum from the trip took him into the defender, Badilla gave the decision in Brazil's favour.

Branco rose to his feet and placed the ball some 30-plus yards from goal, his left foot renowned for its unerring power. In the Dutch goal, de Goey set up a five-man wall hoping that Branco's ball-striking ability would be limited at this late stage in the game. The Fluminense defender strode back marking out a run-up reminiscent of a cricketing fast bowler. He struck the ball with venom, it flew past the wall before swerving in between Romário and Koeman, the former just able to bend his body out of the ball's path. Goalkeeper de Goey scrambled along the line but the ball evaded his dive, striking the left-hand post before crashing into the net.

Brazil had taken a seemingly unassailable 2-0 lead and been clawed back by the opposition yet still managed one final knockout blow to put them into the semi-finals. Now all that stood between them and a place in the final were familiar foes Sweden at Pasadena's Rose Bowl. Despite all of the misgivings, the doubts and questions, Brazil were 90 minutes away from their first World Cup Final since 1970.

The return to California was a welcome one for Brazil, who had yet to concede in the Golden State, Taffarel's goal only being breached in Detroit and Dallas. Sweden had been one of the surprises of the tournament yet on the day they proved nothing other than a mild irritation for an unchanged Brazil who dominated the 90 minutes. Brazil, once more bedecked in their blue away shirts, peppered Ravelli's goal, Romário and Bebeto at their impudent best, combining to wear down a sluggish Sweden side.

The Swedes sat deep hoping to hit Brazil on the counter-attack and utilise the skill and dexterity of Brolin. They created very little and all of the chances fell Brazil's way, Sweden having defender Patrik Andersson to thank for the game remaining goalless at the break. Romário danced between two defenders before he rounded Ravelli only to find the Borussia Mönchengladbach man perfectly placed on the line to block what would have been a certain goal.

The second half brought more of the same. Ravelli tipped over from Zinho before captain and midfield rock Jonas Thern was sent off for what appeared like a stamp on Dunga in the 63rd minute. Colombian referee José Torres Cadena, stationed a mere three yards away from the challenge, was in no mood to quibble with the protesting Swedes and emphatically raised a red card into the air, tilting the balance ever more in Brazil's favour.

The deadlock was finally broken on 80 minutes from the most unlikely of sources. Having tested Ravelli from both distance and close range, a Jorginho cross was sent deep from the right towards the rear of Sweden's six-yard box. Despite their superior height advantage, it was Romário who leapt the highest to head the ball beyond Ravelli. There was no way back for the ten men and Cadena blew the whistle to confirm Brazil would return to Pasadena in four days for the final. Substitute goalkeeper Gilmar draped a Brazil flag over Romário whilst even Parreira allowed himself a brief punch of the air. They were one step closer to becoming *tetracampeão*.

Chapter Sixteen

A Door in the Sky

THE REPETITIVE thud could be heard from the hotel corridor that ran adjacent to a large function room. On the other side of the door, in a space usually reserved for wedding receptions, a solitary figure kicked a ball against the wall. Back and forth, Roberto Baggio continued until he was certain the nagging ache in his hamstring was no more. 'I was desperate to play,' Baggio recalled in his autobiography, *Una Porta Nel Cielo*. 'I would have played even if they had cut my leg off.' He had suffered similar injuries before and had played on, but this wasn't just 'any' game. In a matter of hours, Italy would be going head-to-head with Brazil in the World Cup Final.

In the grand scheme of things, it was no surprise that Brazil and Italy had made yet another final. Both countries had previous; the winners at the Rose Bowl would be lifting their fourth World Cup having combined for an appearance in half of the other 14 finals. They previously met in the 1970 final when the greatest Brazil team to grace the game blew the *Azzurri* away 4-1 in Mexico. Italy learnt their lesson 12 years later when a Brazil side overflowing with flair players was stopped in its tracks as Enzo Bearzot's team crushed the dreams of the Samba Nation on the way to their third title.

'Amongst Brazilian fans there was the atmosphere of a rematch and for the press that was good for selling newspapers,' said Martins. 'It must have been a motivational factor for the players too, but if we analyse it coldly and with distancing no achievement will erase the tragedy of Sarriá in 1982 [where Brazil lost 3-2 to Italy].' Expectations were high in Italy, and there was a strong belief amongst the country's football press that their fourth World Cup would be attained, *Gazzetta dello Sport* particularly confident noting that, 'Brazil don't have a Pelé: we can do it.'

On this occasion the finalists had been pushed all the way in the semi-finals by Sweden and Bulgaria, whose dream runs were ended by two world football superpowers. They were both more than capable of causing an upset and good value for their places in the semi-finals. When the dust settled, however, normal service had been resumed with the European underdogs having to make do with the needless third-place play-off 24 hours before Italy and Brazil met.

The Italians left their base camp in New Jersey and set up training quarters at the Loyola Marymount University in Los Angeles whilst *O Seleção* remained in Los Gatos, having transformed the Bay Area town into a mini Brazil. The day before the final Arrigo Sacchi put his squad through a light training session where Franco Baresi looked back to his best. Baggio, however, remained on the sidelines, desperately testing the reliability of his right hamstring. The Prophet of Fusignano remained tight-lipped on his team selection, though two things were certain with Alessandro Costacurta and Mauro Tassotti both suspended following their respective semi-final misdemeanours. Sacchi tentatively pencilled both Baresi and Roberto Baggio into his starting XI but a final decision on their fitness would go down to the wire. *La Gazzetta dello Sport* had even gone as far as saying that Baresi wouldn't make it with Luigi Apolloni set to deputise. 'The only uncertainties I had were the health of Baresi and Baggio, two very important players,' explained Sacchi. 'The doctors tested them in the morning [of the final] and gave the okay for them to play.'

Sacchi wasn't averse to shuffling the pack to suit his rigid tactics; by either necessity or choice he had used all but two of his squad. At some point during the month-long tournament, it seemed as if every Italian player had been limping. Meanwhile, in the Brazil camp, Carlos Alberto Parreira had only made two changes up to this point. Branco had replaced Leonardo following his dismissal in the USA game and Mazinho had been called upon to replace Raí. In total, 16 of his 22 players had seen action but despite calls to play 17-year-old *wunderkind* Ronaldo, Parreira had generally stood by his players. Neither coach would win popularity contests in their respective countries but with victory here all would be forgotten.

The final saw two teams who were defensively sound, an obvious characteristic at the time of Italian football but a whole new concept to the Brazilians. *O Seleção* had only conceded three goals whilst the *Azzurri*, who looked close to exiting the tournament on more than one occasion, had shipped five. Brazil were unbeaten and at the stage where the overall result far outweighed the performance. Italy had enjoyed their fair share of luck and had shown signs of improvement as they progressed. They would be the first winners since Argentina in 1978 to lift the trophy despite losing a game.

When the teams were announced, Baresi and Baggio were in Sacchi's line-up. Up front Daniele Massaro was preferred to Giuseppe Signori with the Lazio striker kept in reserve should Baggio's hamstring flare up again. Baresi was partnered in the centre of defence by Paolo Maldini whilst the impressive Roberto Mussi and Antonio Benarrivo shored up the flanks. Parreira had the luxury of being able to take his usual approach. The two banks of four would stand guard whilst the creativity and goal threat would come from Bebeto and Romário. The makeshift centre-half pairing of Marcio Santos and Aldair would once again provide the defensive backbone.

The game kicked off at 12.30pm in front of 94,194 fans who crammed into the Rose Bowl in brutally hot conditions. Swathes of yellow, green and blue were evident in the stands as the temperature hit 36°C, so warm that the Brazilians took to the pitch without their usual training jackets. They were also hand in hand, forming a chain and sending a message to their doubters back home; they were one unit, strong, solid and would not be broken. 'This was a perfect synthesis of the Brazilian team. Balanced and assembled with the need to play collectively,' said Martins.

Hungarian referee Sándor Puhl blew his whistle to get the game underway. Like two heavyweight boxers, both teams sounded each other out with neither looking to take any early risks. Following the cautious start, Brazil began to push forward as the midfield looked to guide through-balls to the front two. Any doubts over Baresi were quickly quashed as he snuffed out the Brazilian supply time and again. Wherever Romário went, he was there unwilling to let Brazil's dangerman out of his sight, proving Parreira's point that 'it was better to be injured than tired'.

It wasn't long before the injury curse struck again. First it struck Brazil with Jorginho having to be replaced by a relative unknown outside of South America, Marcos de

Moraes, also known as Cafu. Parreira's decision to bring on the then 25-year-old São Paulo defender began a journey that saw Cafu become the first player to appear in three consecutive World Cup finals. Nine minutes later the Italian defence was snakebitten once more, Mussi unable to continue with Luigi Apolloni joining his Parma team-mate Benarrivo as the opposite full-back.

A half of few chances ended with both sets of players eager to take on fluids and attempt to reinvigorate tired muscles. A combination of the heat, travel and a punishing schedule that saw the semi-finals played only four days earlier put paid to what many hoped would be an open and entertaining final. 'At half time I said, "we need to attack with more players," they replied they couldn't do it, they were too tired,' said Sacchi. 'The will was there, but the East coast had boiled us. We had no time for recovery, at night the heat and air conditioning did not help, we reached the final exhausted,' Sacchi explained.

Roberto Donadoni, having struggled with a hamstring injury of his own in the build-up, told Sacchi at half-time, 'If we go upfield, we're not going to be able to get back.' Put bluntly, both teams looked leggy.

Chances were also at a premium throughout the second half, a Bebeto header comfortably saved by Gianluca Pagliuca being a particular stand out. Baggio had struggled and the injured hamstring was clearly still on his mind. 'Maybe at the beginning of the game, I couldn't let go,' he said in his autobiography. 'Subconsciously I was worried about hurting myself, but after a while I got over that. However, I didn't have a great game and neither did the team.'

With 15 minutes remaining, Pagliuca had his post to thank for the game remaining scoreless when a harmless Mauro Silva effort squirmed through his hands bouncing against the woodwork before going into his grateful arms. The Sampdoria stopper kissed his glove and touched the post, sending a thank you to the heavens in the process. Maybe luck would continue to be on the *Azzurri*'s side.

The game headed for extra time. Baggio left the pitch at the end of 90 gruelling minutes clutching at the back of his right leg, returning with a compression sleeve around his stricken limb. Signori remained on the bench; Baggio was going to see this through to the very end. Cafu continued to show glimpses of what was to come in his illustrious career by repeatedly racing down the right wing. One such run produced Brazil's best chance when his cross found Bebeto who steered the ball across goal for Romário, whose effort was frantically scrambled away by Pagliuca.

Baresi rolled back the years to his time as a *libero*, striding out of defence with the ball at his feet, looking to break through Brazil's solid rearguard. At one point the captain was the furthest Italian up the pitch. There was still time for a glimpse of Baggio magic when, in space, he sent a dipping volley towards the Brazil goal which Taffarel touched over the bar. Cramp and fatigue had set in by now with players digging into their reserves once more. Baresi's body seemed to finally surrender to the punishment as he crashed to the turf in obvious discomfort. Maldini and Apolloni raced to his aid to force his foot back and relieve the tightness in his leg. Brazil certainly seemed the fresher of the two teams. Parreira gave a World Cup debut to striker Viola during extra time with instructions to run at the tiring Italian defence. The Corinthians man caused havoc for 14 minutes, arguably the best of his career, as he failed to hit those heights again.

Eventually, Puhl brought proceedings to an end. After 120 minutes in the early-afternoon Pasadena sun, for the first time ever a World Cup Final would be decided by a penalty shoot-out. Sacchi had taken a risk playing unfit players but the likes of Baggio and Baresi had come through two hours of football, the former practically on one leg whilst the latter endured knee surgery only 25 days earlier. Signori, a more than adept penalty taker for his club side Lazio, would play no part in Italy's second ever penalty shoot-out, the modern trend of specialised players coming from the bench for the shoot-out being unheard of in 1994.

It was a time for heroes. Pagliuca and Taffarel walked down together, friends from their time in Italy, each aware that their nation's destiny was in the lap of the gods.

After 51 matches and 141 goals, it all came down to penalty kicks, perhaps fitting that the World Cup should end as it began as one-month earlier with music royalty Diana Ross' as infamous effort. Baresi made his way from the halfway line, socks rolled down, hair and shirt soaked in sweat. He had scored 33 goals during his legendary playing career, 21 of which had been from the penalty spot. Tired and aching, he desperately tried to shake life into his legs as Taffarel took his place on the line. Baresi later said he originally planned to place the penalty to the Brazilian's left but crucially changed his mind at the last moment, scooping the ball high over the bar.

Brazil failed to take advantage with their first kick as Marcio Santos saw his firm drive pushed away by Pagliuca. The next four all went with the takers; Demetrio Albertini, Romário with his first ever penalty, substitute Alberigo Evani and Branco all converted from the spot to make the shoot-out 2-2. Dunga and Bebeto were still to step up for Brazil whilst Italy had kept strikers Massaro and Baggio until last. Massaro telegraphed a side-footed effort that Taffarel easily rebuffed, and the Brazilian goalkeeper leapt to his feet in triumph, waving a finger in the air.

Now it was the turn of captain Dunga, the face of the new 'anti-*Jogo Bonito*' Brazil. He epitomised the blue-collar, hard-working approach that Parreira had adopted and whilst he may not have had the panache of some of the Brazilian midfielders from yesteryear he was just as vital. He had been brought back into the international fold by Parreira who felt his side was missing the bullish toughness that came with him. Dunga gently placed the ball on the penalty spot and took nine steps back. His strike initially froze Pagliuca, who fell one way with the ball going the other. Advantage Brazil, 3-2.

Italy's hopes rested at the feet of *Il Divin Codino*. Miss and the World Cup was Brazil's. BBC commentator Barry Davies summed it up as Italy's talisman stepped forward: 'All the pressure now on Roberto Baggio,' he said sensing the drama, 'the man who really has brought the team to the final, now has to save them.' The Brazil bench stood in a line. Arms around each other, whilst Parreira couldn't bring himself to look.

The man who came alive in the knockout stages and brought Italy back from the dead time and again had to do it once more. Before the World Cup, Baggio spoke in a rare interview saying when he was a child that he had dreamt of one day scoring in a World Cup Final. Now this was his chance, albeit in a penalty shoot-out. Despite his aching hamstring, Baggio was the team's penalty taker and had done his homework on the Brazil goalkeeper, knowing he always committed to a dive when facing a penalty. The plan was clear in Baggio's mind. Taffarel would dive one way and he would hit the ball down the centre of the goal high enough to evade any of the Brazilian's outstretched limbs.

Just as predicted, Taffarel dived, again to his left. To Baggio's horror, however, he could only watch as his usually obedient right foot betrayed him, sending his effort high into the Pasadena sky. The rays of the cruel California sun beat down on Baggio, who stood transfixed in disbelief, head lowered, with hands on hips. 'The World Cup is over,' Italian commentator Bruno Pizzul opined. 'Brazil win.'

Taffarel was on his knees, eyes closed mouthing thanks to a higher power whilst his team-mates rushed from the halfway line. The Brazilian bench cleared, a member of Parreira's staff acrobatically performing a forward roll on to the pitch. The jubilant Brazilian players hoisted their manager up, throwing him high into the air. Pagliuca buried his face in the Rose Bowl turf as Baresi flopped into the arms of Antonio Mattarese, the FIGC president. A disconsolate Baggio was consoled by numerous team-mates; the moment he had waited his life for was gone. In the stands, Brazilian commentator Gālvao Bueno embraced Pelé as they both repeatedly shouted '*tetra*' in unison. Back on the pitch the Brazilians completed a lap of honour before unfurling a banner in homage to Ayrton Senna as they dedicated their fourth title to the man who died chasing his.

Baggio couldn't explain the miss to the press afterwards. 'I was there in body and spirit for the penalty,' he explained. 'I don't know why I sent it over.' Just how much of an impact did the hamstring injury have on him? Especially when coupled with the weight of expectation he had carried for the previous four weeks? 'I was tired, but I have never run away from my responsibilities,' Baggio wrote in his autobiography. 'Only those who have the courage to take a penalty miss them. I failed that time and it affected me for years. I still dream about it, if I could erase a moment from my career, it would be that one.'

Sacchi was adamant that if he could relive the game again, he wouldn't do anything different, including the shoot-out. 'Taking a penalty in training is not the same as in a match, in training they never missed!'

Dunga lifted the trophy, shouting expletives at the waiting press hordes who had lambasted and doubted this Brazil side. They may not have played the stylish football that the teams of 1970 and 1982 had, but they were World Cup winners, playing Parreira's way. Despite pressure to conform to Brazilian traditions, they had ended 24 years of hurt. 'We did not change anything, because we had a team who knew they would win it,' Parreira said. 'They had that mentality.'

Over two decades later, Sacchi was philosophical in defeat. 'I thanked the players, they had shown great will and professionalism,' said the man who led AC Milan to back-to-back European Cup victories. It was an opinion he held at the time too. 'Everybody has done their best, it was a brutal battle, but everybody gave everything he had to give,' he shrugged to the press after the final.

A disconsolate Baggio scooped his young daughter up in his arms as he waited to board the team bus outside the Rose Bowl. Desperate for normality he headed to Argentina and took refuge with his family at his newly acquired ranch in La Pampa.

Later that summer Italian newspaper *La Repubblica* spoke of 'the physical and philosophical limits of a young man used as a totem and talisman, a champion of whom too much has to be asked'. Baggio's career had brought ample physical pain, but this was different, maybe this wound would never heal. The sometimes-vitriolic Italian football press showed compassion for their talisman and his team. Baggio, along with Baresi, had played through the pain barrier to take Italy the farthest in a World Cup since the one they won in 1982. The *Azzurri*'s spirit and effort could not be questioned; they had overcome injuries to key men and came within a penalty shoot-out of winning their fourth title.

'There was great disappointment in the defeat, but also a lot of pride,' said the suspended Costacurta. Losing to Brazil also held no shame, although questions were asked of why FIFA held one semi-final on the east coast (Bulgaria v Italy) whilst *O Seleção* had the luxury of avoiding a 3,000-mile trip by playing their final two games at the Rose Bowl.

Parties continued throughout the night in Brazil as the day after the final victory was declared a national holiday. The 1994 winners lacked the playmaking skills of the 1982 side but made up for that with the commodities that Telê Santana's side severely lacked, a potent strike force and a strong defence.

The drama didn't end here. Brazilian newspaper *Folha de S.Paulo* reported rows at the airport when the squad returned home with 15 tons more luggage than they left with. The generous exchange rate saw a plethora of electronics and home appliances make the journey from the USA to Brazil, with one unnamed player transporting a whole kitchen on a separate flight, causing headaches for the federal government in Brasilia.

In footballing terms, however, Parreira had thumbed his nose at the 150 million coaches he spoke of back home. Answering his critics, he got out on top, returning to club football with Valencia in Spain shortly after the finals. Brazil's fourth World Cup title had been a long time coming but finally they had company for the Jules Rimet Trophy they kept following their third victory way back in 1970.

The goal in the USA that summer was to win by any means necessary. For Parreira, his staff and squad, it was mission accomplished.

Chapter Seventeen

Mission Accomplished

AFTER 52 games across 31 days, the 1994 World Cup was over. Figuratively, Alan Rothenberg's plan to put on the 'greatest show on Earth' appeared to have come true. An estimated two billion people watched the final on television with over 94,000 in attendance at the Rose Bowl, an amount that has not been matched since. A total of 3,597,042 people had attended games across the USA, over a million more than in Italy four years earlier.

The average attendance of 68,991 was also a record as crowds appeared unperturbed by mercury-melting temperatures and gave a slap in the face to all those who doubted the interest was there. An explosion in the growth of World Cup finances started and continued to the point where revenue for the 2018 World Cup rose by 25 per cent to almost £6bn.

There were goals aplenty with FIFA's decision to alter the offside laws paying dividends; the huge nets bulged 26 more times than at Italia 90. There were also fewer 1-0 victories whilst the amount of dreaded 0-0 draws was also down, something for those who judged the quality of the tournament only by the final to bear in mind.

The new rules that referees put into practice did see an increase in the number of yellow cards issued, a clear sign that the game was moving towards protecting attacking players more. This in turn gave rise to a plethora of individual stars to emerge in the next decade, particularly Lionel Messi and Cristiano Ronaldo, whose generational talents would elevate the game to stratospheric levels.

Romário took home the Golden Ball award for the best player at the tournament whilst Hristo Stoichkov and Oleg Salenko shared the Golden Boot as top goalscorers, the Russian bagging five of his six goals in the dead rubber with Cameroon.

The final, derided for its lack of action, collapsed under its own weight of expectancy and a level of hype that it was never going to live up to. The cruel kick-off time that pandered to European audiences coupled with the caution of the respective coaches helped produce a stultifying stalemate. More than two decades later the trend continues with top-flight managers regularly bemoaning the schedule set by TV networks. The early kick-off times after a Wednesday-night Champions League game were commonplace with the TV companies eager to wring every ounce out of their investment, the Premier League only implementing a rule change to stop this in 2021. Whilst their influence is unwelcomed, it is a necessary evil for clubs as the vast sums make up a huge part of their finances in the 21st century.

The conditions, temperatures and travel had taken their toll on the players, many of whom were ready to go home, not play in a World Cup Final. What a further three days' rest would have done for the spectacle is up for conjecture, but the scheduling would not allow it. Players needed holidays before the throes of the European leagues began in earnest the following month. Some precautions against burnout were taken. The English Premier League was still in its infancy in 1994. It was agreed that the 1993/94 season would end early to allow players adequate time to rest before joining up with England ahead of USA 94, only for the Three Lions to miss out on qualification altogether. Stung by this embarrassing failure, it took until the 2019/20 season for the Premier League to follow their European neighbours in allowing a mid-season break, only for the Covid-19 pandemic to cause all leagues to be suspended shortly after.

When it came to the 1994 World Cup, time was of the essence to maximise the world's focus and attention. It was deemed the tournament had to be done and dusted in a month, no way to treat what is arguably the greatest sporting event in the world, but the results speak for themselves. The 2018 World Cup attendance figures got close to but failed to surpass those of USA 94, even with the introduction of more teams (32) which began in 1998. Was it a case of US sports fans' love for a big event or something more? Its nearest competitor, the Olympic Games, arrived in the USA two summers later with supporters yet again coming out in force as they bought some 8.3 million tickets.

That same year the big test of whether the USA had got to grips with the 'beautiful game' arrived with the debut of Major League Soccer (MLS). The professional league that was promised back in 1988 finally emerged to much fanfare although an average attendance of 17,406 for the inaugural season showed that perhaps the interest gained in 1994 had begun to wane.

The David Beckham effect provided a shot in the arm when he joined Los Angeles Galaxy in 2007 and helped to secure TV deals around the world. The MLS had gained an unfortunate reputation for being a retirement home for European players, but it has since found itself as a popular next step on a starlet's football journey. The MLS has experienced a slow burn over the previous two decades, with proof of its progress in the movement of some of its homegrown talent to several top European clubs. In 2019 researchers from the CIES Football Observatory within the International Centre for Sports Studies in Switzerland found that in 51 national leagues, the second-greatest increase in crowds came in the MLS. Between 2003 and 2008 the average crowd at an MLS game was 15,920, but from 2013 to 2018 it rose 34 per cent to 21,358.

Without the 1994 World Cup profits, it's likely MLS would have struggled to get off the ground. The USA was the first country to benefit from the huge amounts of money that hosting the World Cup generates. Total tournament revenue was counted at $350m with some $60m profit, double what Rothenberg and US Soccer expected. The profits were put to use and an influx of stars from that tournament raised the media profile of the league. Many of the players who starred for the hosts returned home whilst the likes of Jorge Campos, Roberto Donadoni, Alain Sutter, Carlos Valderrama, Marco Etcheverry and Hristo Stoichkov all played in the nascent MLS, adding to its hopes for respectability.

The profits continued to pay dividends when in 1999 and again in 2003 (at short notice due to the SARS crisis rendering China's hosting impossible) the USA hosted two Women's World Cups with the former proving to be the most successful in terms of attendance, television ratings and public interest. The US women's team currently leads the way in terms of tournament victories with Brandi Chastain and Megan Rapinoe placed alongside Mia Hamm in the public consciousness as the women's game continues to grow exponentially throughout the world.

Financially, the 1994 World Cup was a watershed moment. The Brazilian Football Confederation took advantage of the national team's status as world champions when they signed a record £100m kit deal with Nike in 1996. The details of the deal would be highlighted after the final of France 98, which led to question marks over how much of a hold the global company had over Brazilian football. Brazil's success extended beyond finances, however. 'In my opinion, that victory [in 1994] saved Brazilian football. It kickstarted a new era,' left-back Leonardo told FIFA.com ahead of the 2006 World Cup. 'Seriously 24 years without a trophy is an enormous weight on anyone's shoulders and things definitely got easier for Brazilian footballers after this.' This much was true. In 1994, only Romário was playing at one of Europe's big clubs. The World Cup win helped restore faith in the Brazilian footballer and paved the way for the likes of Ronaldo and Ronaldinho to join the European elite.

European football too was changing, with clubs in England breaking away to form the English Premier League in 1992. The early TV coverage boasted cheerleaders and fireworks which had the British press clutching their pearls at the thought of the game changing, arguably fuelling the animosity towards the USA as World Cup hosts. New revenue streams from the £304m BSkyB deal opened the door for clubs to sign more illustrious players, with many arriving after showcasing their talents at the World Cup. By 2019 this deal had grown to an estimated £5bn with Serie A, La Liga and the Bundesliga also securing deals of between £2bn and £4bn respectively.

The changes were coming thick and fast with the entire transfer system shaken to its core in 1995 when lower-league Belgian footballer Jean-Marc Bosman took football to court and won. The landmark legal ruling allowed for players to move freely within the European Union once their contracts had expired whilst also putting an end to foreign-player quotas that teams had been working under.

How people consumed the game was also in a state of flux in these pre-internet days. From 1954 (when the first World Cup matches were broadcast) to 1986, *Time* magazine estimated that the number of television sets worldwide had grown from 30 million to more than 650 million. Until 1994, football in the USA was predominantly shown on Univision, the Spanish-language network. Backed by corporate sponsors, US TV networks beamed live games into homes for the first time since 1986, with ABC averaging a Nielsen rating of 5.3, up 18 per cent from predictions at the beginning of the tournament. The Nielsen rating shows the percentage of TV-owning households in the nation combined with how many had their sets turned on. Each point equates to around 940,000 homes and the previous record was 6.6, from when Italy and Germany met in the 1982 World Cup.

The record was broken several times during 1994, clearly helped by the performance of the host nation, with their second-round loss to Brazil achieving a Nielsen rating of 9.3, only narrowly beaten by the final. The OJ Simpson police chase also highlighted the power of a live televised news story which had the nation gripped, thankfully for organisers not at the same time as the opening ceremony or first game. Quite what Sky Sports News, which launched its 24-hour cycle in 1998, would have made of it is anyone's guess, but if its excessive transfer-deadline coverage is anything to go by one can only imagine.

Football fans stateside now have wall-to-wall access to all the biggest and best leagues on offer, whilst the MLS has also secured overseas broadcast deals, two scenarios which would have seemed alien in the Werner Fricker days. The growth of the Champions League has seen it become the premier club competition with its TV deal in the UK alone commanding a cool £1.2bn.

Whilst it remains obvious that the globalisation of football seemed inevitable, the 1994 World Cup showcased the ease with which sponsors could get their brand name in front of millions of prospective customers without having to use the USA's tried and trusted tactic of numerous commercial breaks during the coverage. It also uncovered the sheer amount of money people were willing to spend to get their hands on a ticket or memento, with the USA 94 logo or mascot, Striker the World Cup Pup, emblazoned on any and every item you could imagine.

Football is now big business in the States, with a quarter of 2020 English Premier League clubs having some form of US ownership. The trickle-down effect is evident too with former Disney CEO Michael Eisner's Tornante Company buying Portsmouth FC from its supporters' trust in 2017. Hollywood stars Rob McElhenney and Ryan Reynolds emerged in 2020 as the surprise owners of National League side Wrexham AFC, the duo drawn in by the history and community spirit of Wales's oldest professional club. In turn, dozens of European clubs traverse the Atlantic Ocean every summer to press the flesh of their American fans before returning home to complain about the lack of recovery time due to the number of games on their schedule.

Many people can pinpoint the 1994 World Cup as the seminal moment that helped them fall in love with 'the beautiful game', but in the USA it also proved to have a beneficial effect on the future of the national team. Subsequent stars of the US national team – Tim Howard,

Michael Bradley, Graham Zusi, Landon Donovan and Clint Dempsey – all speak about how USA 94 gave them the belief and push to make it in the professional game. Dempsey, who grew up in a Texas trailer park and spent his formative years playing the game with his Mexican immigrant neighbours, was thrilled upon hearing his hero, Diego Maradona, would be playing in the nearby Cotton Bowl only for his dream to be dashed by the Argentine's suspension. Dempsey went on to join Tottenham Hotspur for a then-record $9.6m and became, to date, the only American to score a Premier League hat-trick.

USA 94 signalled the beginning of FIFA's empire-building quest which extended to Africa in 2010, then to the Middle East in 2022. This translated into huge financial success for FIFA; despite the many corruption controversies that beset world football's governing body, revenues from the 2018 World Cup in Russia hit $5.4bn with more than $3.5bn profit. In 2026 the competition will finally return to the Americas after a joint bid from Canada, Mexico and the USA was accepted.

Italia 90 provided a glimpse at what football could achieve. It unlocked a door that had been padlocked by stadium disasters and hooliganism. The 1994 World Cup not only opened the door, but smashed it off its hinges. The genie was out of the bottle and football was on its way to becoming the global force that it is today. Whether that is a good thing or not I'll leave for you to decide, but the impact of the tournament is unquestionable.

Group Results and Final Standings

Group A
USA 1-1 Switzerland
Colombia 1-3 Romania
Romania 1-4 Switzerland
USA 2-1 Colombia
USA 0-1 Romania
Switzerland 0-2 Colombia
1. Romania 6
2. Switzerland 4
3. USA 4
4. Colombia 3

Group B
Cameroon 2-2 Sweden
Brazil 2-0 Russia
Brazil 3-0 Cameroon
Sweden 3-1 Russia
Russia 6-1 Cameroon
Brazil 1-1 Sweden
1. Brazil 7
2. Sweden 5
3. Russia 3
4. Cameroon 1

Group C
Germany 1-0 Bolivia
Spain 2-2 South Korea
Germany 1-1 Spain
South Korea 0-0 Bolivia
Bolivia 1-3 Spain
Germany 3-2 South Korea
1. Germany 7
2. Spain 5
3. South Korea 2
4. Bolivia 1

Group D
Argentina 4-0 Greece
Nigeria 3-0 Bulgaria
Argentina 2-1 Nigeria
Bulgaria 4-0 Greece
Greece 0-2 Nigeria
Argentina 0-2 Bulgaria
1. Nigeria 6
2. Bulgaria 6
3. Argentina 6
4. Greece 0

Group E
Italy 0-1 Rep of Ireland
Norway 1-0 Mexico
Italy 1-0 Norway
Mexico 2-1 Rep of Ireland
Italy 1-1 Mexico
Rep of Ireland 0-0 Norway
1. Mexico 4
2. Italy 4
3. Rep of Ireland 4
4. Norway 4

Group F
Belgium 1-0 Morocco
Netherlands 2-1 Saudi Arabia
Belgium 1-0 Netherlands
Saudi Arabia 2-1 Morocco
Belgium 0-1 Saudi Arabia
Morocco 1-2 Netherlands
1. Netherlands 6
2. Saudi Arabia 6
3. Belgium 6
4. Morocco 0

Knockout Stages
Round of 16
Germany 3-2 Belgium
Spain 3-0 Switzerland
Saudi Arabia 1-3 Sweden
Romania 3-2 Argentina

Netherlands 2-0 Republic of Ireland
Brazil 1-0 USA
Nigeria 1-2 Italy (after extra time)
Mexico 1-1 Bulgaria (1-3 penalties)

Quarter-Finals   *Semi-Finals*
Italy 2-1 Spain   Bulgaria 1-2 Italy
Netherlands 2-3 Brazil   Sweden 0-1 Brazil
Bulgaria 2-1 Germany
Romania 2-2 Sweden (4-5 penalties)

Third-place play-off   *Final*
Sweden 4-0 Bulgaria   Brazil 0-0 Italy (3-2 penalties)

The Stats and Numbers

Matches Played: 52
Goals Scored: 141 (2.71 per match)
Yellow Cards: 235
Red Cards: 15
Total Attendance: 3,597,042
Golden Boot: Hristo Stoichkov (Bulgaria) & Oleg Salenko (Russia) 6
Bronze Shoe: Romário (Brazil) & Kennet Andersson (Sweden)
Golden Ball: Romário (Brazil)
Silver Ball: Roberto Baggio (Italy)
Bronze Ball: Hristo Stoichkov (Bulgaria)
Fair Play Award: Brazil
Most Entertaining Team: Brazil
Best Young Player Award: Marc Overmars (Netherlands)
Yashin Award for Best Goalkeeper: Michel Preud'homme (Belgium)

All-Star Team

Goalkeeper: Michel Preud'homme (Belgium)
Defenders: Jorginho (Brazil), Marcio Santos (Brazil), Paolo Maldini (Italy)
Midfielders: Dunga (Brazil), Krasimir Balakov (Bulgaria), Gheorghe Hagi (Romania), Tomas Brolin (Sweden)
Forwards: Romário (Brazil), Hristo Stoichkov (Bulgaria), Roberto Baggio (Italy)

Acknowledgements

WRITING THIS book has easily been one of the most surreal moments of my life. I have been absolutely blown away by all of the help I have received whether it's a suggestion, an interview, a contact or someone taking their time to reply to emails or pass on a message. Every single one has contributed in some way and without them this book would not have been possible.

Firstly, I'd like to thank everyone at Pitch Publishing for not only believing in the idea but also for believing in me as a writer. Having that faith in my idea helped me push on when the words weren't flowing and I will be forever grateful.

Thank you also to my wife Lindsey who gave me the space, time and encouragement whenever needed. Lindsey was always there to lend an ear and having her behind me spurred me on even more. Thanks also go to my three amazing sons, Noah, Flynn and Jude; without them the book would have been finished a lot sooner!

Also, a big thank you to Daniel Williamson whose proof reading, advice, support and daily messages made the process all the more enjoyable, and Lee Wynne, whose keen eye for detail was as greatly received as the support he provided throughout. Also, to Steven Scragg whose early encouragement was invaluable.

The numerous messages, suggestions, ideas and memories that people sent me via Twitter showed me there are like-minded souls out there who hold the 1994 World Cup as close to their heart as I do. A special thank you must go to Jim Trecker, whose depth of knowledge and contacts really got the ball rolling back in the early days of writing the book.

Thank you to those who shared memories of their involvement with the tournament. Hank Steinbrecher, Alan Rothenberg, Matt Lorenzo, Bob Wilson, John Helm, Roger Twibell, Seamus Malin, Frits Barend, George Vecsey, Thom Meredith, Professor Trey Rogers and Phil Schoen all very kindly gave up their time to speak with me.

Thanks also go to Tim Vickery, Patricio Córdoba, Marluci Martins and Pieter Stroink van Eizenga who provided and set up some of the first interviews I undertook back in early 2020. Also, to the players and coaches who helped make the World Cup what it was: Mike Sorber, Alexi Lalas, Marcelo Balboa, Clemens Westerhof, Mutiu Adepoju, Bryan Roy, Andreas Brehme, Rainer Bonhof, Óscar Ruggeri, Tsanko Tsvetanov, Saeed Al-Owairan, Ioan Lupescu, Thomas Ravelli, Arrigo Sacchi and Alessandro Costacurta. Their words are all included in the book.

I would also like to thank Carl Worswick, Uli Hesse, Wael Jabir, David Winner, Emanuele Giulianelli, James Campbell Taylor, Andres Burgo, Igor Siqueira, Márvio dos Anjos and anyone else who has helped me throughout this process, no matter how small, it means so much. I finally want to thank everyone who has bought, read and supported this book. I hope you all get as much joy from reading this book as I did from researching and writing it.

Bibliography

Books

Agnew, P., *Forza Italia* (Ebury Press 2007)

Baggio, R., *Una Porta Nel Cielo* (Limina 2001)

Bellos, A., *Futebol* (Bloomsbury 2014)

Bergkamp, D. and Winner, D., *Stillness and Speed* (Simon & Schuster 2014)

Byrne, P. and Charlton, J., *Jack Charlton's American World Cup Diary* (BCA 1994)

Campomar, A., *Golazo!* (Quercus Editions 2014)

Cox, M., *The Mixer* (HarperCollins 2018)

Foot, J., *Calcio* (Fourth Estate 2006)

Galeano, E., *Football in Sun and Shadow* (Fourth Estate 2003)

Glanville, B., *The Story of the World Cup* (Faber & Faber 2018)

Goldblatt, D., *Futebol Nation* (Penguin 2014)

Goldblatt, D., *The Ball Is Round* (Penguin 2007)

Hesse, U., *Tor!* (WSC Books 2003)

Horton, E., *The Best World Cup Money Can Buy* (Ed Horton 1995)

Keane, R., *Keane* (Penguin 2011)

Kuper, S. and Szymanski, S., *Soccernomics* (HarperSport 2014)

Lever, J., *Soccer Madness* (University of Chicago Press 1984)

Maradona, D., *El Diego* (Yellow Jersey Press 2005)

Redhead, S., *Post Fandom and the Millennial Blues* (Routledge 1997)
Vecsey, G., *Eight World Cups* (St Martin's Griffin 2015)
Wangerin, D., *Soccer in a Football World* (WSC Books 2006)
Watson, D., *Dancing in the Streets* (Victor Gollancz 1994)
Wilson, J., *Angels with Dirty Faces* (Orion 2016)
Wilson, J., *Inverting the Pyramid* (Orion 2014)
Winner, D., *Brilliant Orange* (Bloomsbury 2001)

Websites
90Min.com
ArabNews.com
BackpageFootball.com
BaltimoreSun.com
BBC.co.uk
CoachesVoice.com
Courant.com
DailyRecord.co.uk
Deseret.com
Duke.edu
ESPN.com
EveningExpress.co.uk
FAI.ie
FIFA.com
Footballia.net
Football-Italia.net
FootballWhispers.com
Forbes.com
FourFourTwo.com
GentlemanUltra.com
Goal.com
HuffPost.com
LATimes.com
MercuryNews.com

NYTimes.com
OTBSports.com
PlanetFootball.com
PlanetWorldCup.com
Reuters.com
SI.com
SoccerAmerica.com
Sportico.com
Telegraph.co.uk
TheBlizzard.co.uk
TheGuardian.com
TheIndependent.co.uk
TheJournal.ie
TheNationalNews.com
TheNewFederalist.eu
TheseFootballTimes.co.uk
WashingtonPost.com
WorldFinance.com
WorldFootballIndex.com
WSC.co.uk

Also available at all good book stores

9781801501149

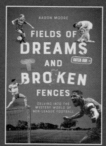

9781801501002

9781801500739

9781801500876

9781801500906

9781801500913

9781801500692

9781801501323

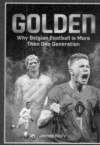

9781801501057